D1098145

To:

Patricia

From:

Love
Mary Lynne

Date:

2. 23. 09

# Nearer to Jesus

## Sarah Young

AUTHOR OF *Jesus Calling*

## THOMAS NELSON
### Since 1798

NASHVILLE   DALLAS   MEXICO CITY   RIO DE JANEIRO   BEIJING

Published in Nashville, Tennessee, by Thomas Nelson.
Thomas Nelson is a registered trademark of Thomas Nelson, Inc.

Thomas Nelson, Inc., titles may be purchased in bulk for educational,
business, fund-raising, or sales promotional use. For information,
please e-mail SpecialMarkets@ThomasNelson.com.

Song lyrics: "Nearer, My God, to Thee" by Sarah F. Adams.
"Nearer, Still Nearer" by Leila N. Morris.

Portions of this book have been previously published in *Jesus Calling*
© 2004 by Sarah Young and *Dear Jesus* © 2007 by Sarah Young.

Unless otherwise indicated, Scripture quotations are taken from the
*New International Version* © 1984 by the International Bible Society.
Used by permission of Zondervan Bible Publishers.

Other Scripture quotations are taken from the *New American Standard Bible* (NASB)
© 1960, 1962, 1963, 1971, 1972, 1973, 1975, and 1977 by the Lockman Foundation.
Used by permission. The *Amplified*® *Bible* (AMP) © 1954, 1958, 1962, 1964, 1965, 1987
by The Lockman Foundation. Used by permission. The *New King James Version* (NKJV)
©1979, 1980, 1982, 1992, Thomas Nelson, Inc. The King James Version (KJV).

ISBN: 978-1-4041-1386-2

*Printed in the United States of America*

08 09 10 11 12 LB 9 8 7 6 5 4 3 2 1

# Introduction

"*Nearer, my God, to Thee, nearer to Thee!*" Doesn't this express the cry of our hearts for nearness to Jesus? But this is only the first line of Sarah Adams' beloved hymn. Here is the second: "*Even though it be a cross that raiseth me . . .*" Often it *is* a cross of suffering that raises us nearer to Jesus. Many of the countless communications I've received from readers deal with suffering—their own and others'. Evidently, God is using *Jesus Calling* and *Dear Jesus* to strengthen, encourage, and comfort people in the throes of adversity.

Both *Jesus Calling* and *Dear Jesus* grew out of my longing to draw closer to my living God. The writings in these books emerged during times of focused concentration on Jesus: waiting in His Presence, listening in my mind for His communications. While listening and writing, I continually asked for the help of the Holy Spirit, who guides my thinking as I listen in Christ's Presence. I've tried to ensure that my writings are consistent with the Bible, the only infallible Word of God.

I wrote the devotions in *Jesus Calling* from the perspective of Jesus speaking to the reader. The devotions in *Dear Jesus* are structured in a dialogue format: the first and third sections are written from the perspective of Jesus speaking; the second section consists of prayers to Him.

*Nearer to Jesus* is a creative compilation of devotions from these two books—containing favorite selections of mine. Each week's readings include one entry from *Dear Jesus* and seven from *Jesus Calling*. The prayers in *Dear Jesus* are meant to open your heart to the *Jesus Calling* devotions that follow.

If we desire to draw nearer to Jesus, we must learn to live in the present moment—for this is where He meets us. As soon as our minds meander into the future or the past, our connection with Him grows weaker. If we linger there, our awareness of His Presence becomes increasingly dim.

The best way I've found to live more fully in the present is to direct my thoughts toward Jesus. My prayers need not be articulate or lengthy, but they must be genuine. As I honestly face my circumstances here and now, I invite Him to enter into them. I bring Him whatever I am doing, thinking, feeling; and I find Him near me—helpfully involved in my situation.

My hope is that *Nearer to Jesus* will help you live close to our Savior—in the present—inviting Him into more and more of your moments. I support you with my prayers, praying in-depth each morning for all the readers of my books. I consider this a delightful privilege and responsibility. May you enjoy bountiful blessings as you grow nearer and nearer to Jesus.

*Sarah Young*

# Nearer, Still Nearer

**A hymn by Leila N. Morris**

Nearer, still nearer, close to Thy heart,
Draw me, my Savior, so precious Thou art;
Fold me, O fold me close to Thy breast,
Shelter me safe in that haven of rest,
Shelter me safe in that haven of rest.

Nearer, still nearer, nothing I bring,
Naught as an off'ring to Jesus my King;
Only my sinful, now contrite heart,
Grant me the cleansing Thy blood doth impart,
Grant me the cleansing Thy blood doth impart.

Nearer, still nearer, Lord, to be Thine,
Sin, with its follies, I gladly resign;
All of its pleasures, pomp and its pride,
Give me but Jesus, my Lord crucified,
Give me but Jesus, My Lord crucified.

Nearer, still nearer, while life shall last,
Till safe in glory my anchor is cast;
Thro' endless ages, ever to be,
Nearer, my Savior, still nearer to Thee,
Nearer, my Savior, still nearer to Thee.

# Week 1

> I, the Lover of your soul, understand you
> perfectly and love you eternally.

## Dear Jesus,

I'm thankful it is my soul You love, rather than my appearance or performance. So often, I'm dissatisfied with both of these, especially when I make them my focus. I'm grateful for Your perfect understanding, since I sometimes feel misunderstood or simply overlooked. Help me experience more fully Your compassionate, unfailing Love.

Beloved, relax in My loving Presence. Let the Light of My Love soak into your entire being. Rest deeply while I massage your thoughts and feelings, helping you change your focus from yourself to Me. *Cease striving and know that I am God.* I created you to know Me: to enjoy Me and center your life in Me.

The world abounds with idols—things you turn to when you want to feel better about yourself: eating, entertainment, exercise, mastery of something or someone. However, none of these things can slake the thirst of your soul, which yearns for Me alone. Idolatrous substitutes may suppress your appetite for Me, mainly by distracting you, but they provide no satisfaction. When you get that gnawing sensation around the edges of your soul, return to Me. Your soul will be satisfied as with the richest of foods.

"Though the mountains be shaken and the hills be removed, yet my unfailing love for you will not be shaken nor my covenant of peace be removed," says the LORD, who has compassion on you.

*Isaiah 54:10*

Cease striving and know that I am God; I will be exalted among the nations, I will be exalted in the earth.

*Psalm 46:10 NASB*

O God, you are my God, earnestly I seek you; my soul thirsts for you... I have seen you in the sanctuary and beheld your power and your glory. Because your love is better than life, my lips will glorify you. I will praise you as long as I live, and in your name I will lift up my hands. My soul will be satisfied as with the richest of foods; with singing lips my mouth will praise you.

*Psalm 63:1–5*

*Sunday*

I want you to experience the riches of your salvation: the Joy of being loved constantly and perfectly. You make a practice of judging yourself, based on how you look or behave or feel. If you like what you see in the mirror, you feel a bit more worthy of My Love. When things are going smoothly and your performance seems adequate, you find it easier to believe you are My beloved child. When you feel discouraged, you tend to look inward so you can correct whatever is wrong.

Instead of trying to "fix" yourself, *fix your gaze on Me, the Lover of your soul.* Rather than using your energy to judge yourself, redirect it to praising Me. Remember that I see you clothed in My righteousness, radiant in My perfect Love.

*Ephesians 2:7–8; Hebrews 3:1; Psalm 34:5*

## Monday

Worship Me only. Idolatry has always been the downfall of My people. I make no secrets about being *a jealous God*. Current idols are more subtle than ancient ones, because today's false gods are often outside the field of religion. People, possessions, status, and self-aggrandizement are some of the most popular deities today. Beware of bowing down before these things. False gods never satisfy; instead, they stir up lust for more and more.

When you seek Me instead of the world's idols, you experience My Joy and Peace. These intangibles slake the thirst of your soul, providing deep satisfaction. The glitter of the world is tinny and temporal. The Light of My Presence is brilliant and everlasting. Walk in the Light with Me. Thus you become a beacon through whom others are drawn to Me.

*Exodus 20:4-5; 2 Samuel 22:29*

*Tuesday*

Learn to live from your true Center in Me. I reside in the deepest depths of your being, in eternal union with your spirit. It is at this deep level that My Peace reigns continually. You will not find lasting peace in the world around you, in circumstances, or in human relationships. The external world is always in flux–under the curse of death and decay. But there is a gold mine of Peace deep within you, waiting to be tapped. Take time to delve into the riches of My residing Presence. I want you to live increasingly from your real Center, where My Love has an eternal grip on you. *I am Christ in you, the hope of Glory.*

Colossians 3:15; Colossians 1:27

## Wednesday

Let Me bless you with My grace and Peace. Open your heart and mind to receive all that I have for you. Do not be ashamed of your emptiness. Instead, view it as the optimal condition for being filled with My Peace.

It is easy to touch up your outward appearance, to look as if you have it all together. Your attempts to look good can fool most people. But I see straight through you, into the depths of your being. There is no place for pretense in your relationship with Me. Rejoice in the relief of being fully understood. Talk with Me about your struggles and feelings of inadequacy. Little by little, I will transform your weaknesses into strengths. Remember that your relationship with Me is saturated in grace. Therefore, *nothing that you do or don't do can separate you from My Presence.*

1 Samuel 16:7; Romans 8:38–39

*Thursday*

Softly I announce My Presence. Shimmering hues of radiance tap gently at your consciousness, seeking entrance. Though I have all Power in heaven and on earth, I am infinitely tender with you. The weaker you are, the more gently I approach you. Let your weakness be a door to My Presence. Whenever you feel inadequate, remember that I am your *ever-present Help*.

Hope in Me, and you will be protected from depression and self-pity. Hope is like a golden cord connecting you to heaven. The more you cling to this cord, the more I bear the weight of your burdens; thus, you are lightened. Heaviness is not of My kingdom. Cling to hope, and My rays of Light will reach you through the darkness.

**Psalm 46:1; Romans 12:12; Romans 15:13**

# Friday

I continually call you to closeness with Me. I know the depth and breadth of your need for Me. I can read the emptiness of your thoughts when they wander away from Me. I offer rest for your soul, as well as refreshment for your mind and body. As you increasingly find fulfillment in Me, other pleasures become less important. Knowing Me intimately is like having a private wellspring of Joy within you. This spring flows freely from My throne of grace, so your Joy is independent of circumstances.

Waiting in My Presence keeps you connected to Me, aware of all that I offer you. If you feel any deficiency, you need to refocus your attention on Me. This is how you trust Me in the moments of your life.

*Psalm 131:2; Psalm 21:6; Psalm 37:7*

*Saturday*

As you turn your attention to Me, feel the Light of My Presence shining upon you. Open your mind and heart to receive My heavenly smile of approval. Let My gold-tinged Love wash over you and soak into the depths of your being. As you are increasingly filled with My Being, you experience joyous union with Me: *I in you, and you in Me.* Your Joy-in-Me and My Joy-in-you become intertwined and inseparable. I suffuse your soul with Joy in My Presence; *at My right hand there are pleasures forevermore.*

*John 17:20–23; Psalm 16:11 (NKJV)*

# Week 2

Do not seek approval in the mirror
or in the eyes of other people.
In My Presence you have infinite approval.

## Dear Jesus,

It's so easy for me to judge myself on the basis
of what I see in the mirror. I know that is fickle and
shallow, because my mirror-image is always changing.
I'm equally enslaved to viewing myself through the eyes
of other people. I tend to evaluate my interpersonal
performance rigorously, and I am almost always
displeased with something I have said or done.
I desperately desire to experience Your approval!

Beloved, "enslaved" is an appropriate word to use.
You are indeed a slave when you try to see and judge
yourself through people's eyes. Evaluating your worth
on the basis of how you look, to yourself or to others,
is always a trap. It's as if you are sifting sand, searching
for gold—yet looking only at the grains of sand filtering
through the sieve, ignoring the gold nuggets that remain.

The gold represents the eternal part of you: your soul. It is invisible to everyone but Me, the One who plans to spend eternity with you. Though invisible, a well-nurtured soul can actually improve your appearance: As you rest in the certainty of My unfailing Love, your face glows with the Joy of My Presence.

My approval of you is infinite because it will continue forever. It is based entirely on My righteousness, which is yours for all eternity. When you look in a mirror, try to see yourself as you truly are—arrayed in perfect righteousness, adorned in glowing approval.

Satisfy us in the morning with your unfailing love,
that we may sing for joy and be glad all our days.
*Psalm 90:14*

Surely you have granted him eternal blessings
and made him glad with the joy of your presence.
*Psalm 21:6*

I delight greatly in the LORD; my soul rejoices in my God.
For he has clothed me with garments of salvation and
arrayed me in a robe of righteousness, as a bridegroom
adorns his head like a priest, and as a bride adorns
herself with her jewels.
*Isaiah 61:10*

*Sunday*

Beware of seeing yourself through other people's eyes. There are several dangers to this practice. First of all, it is nearly impossible to discern what others actually think of you. Moreover, their views of you are variable: subject to each viewer's spiritual, emotional, and physical condition. The major problem with letting others define you is that it borders on idolatry. Your concern to please others dampens your desire to please Me, your Creator.

It is much more real to see yourself through *My eyes*. My gaze upon you is steady and sure, untainted by sin. Through My eyes you can see yourself as one who is deeply, eternally loved. Rest in My loving gaze, and you will receive deep Peace. Respond to My loving Presence by *worshiping Me in spirit and in truth*.

*Hebrews 11:6; John 4:23–24*

## Monday

Open your mind and heart—your entire being—to receive My Love in full measure. So many of My children limp through their lives starved for Love, because they haven't learned the art of receiving. This is essentially an act of faith: believing that I love you with boundless, everlasting Love. The art of receiving is also a discipline: training your mind to trust Me, coming close to Me with confidence.

Remember that the evil one is *the father of lies*. Learn to recognize his deceptive intrusions into your thoughts. One of his favorite deceptions is to undermine your confidence in My unconditional Love. Fight back against these lies! Do not let them go unchallenged. *Resist the devil in My Name, and he will slink away from you. Draw near to Me*, and My Presence will envelop you in Love.

*Ephesians 3:16–19; Hebrews 4:14–16;*
*John 8:44; James 4:7–8 (NKJV)*

*Tuesday*

Rest in the deep assurance of My unfailing Love. Let your body, mind, and spirit relax in My Presence. Release into My care anything that is troubling you, so that you can focus your full attention on Me. Be awed by the vast dimensions of My Love for you: *wider, longer, higher, and deeper* than anything you know. Rejoice that this marvelous Love is yours forever!

The best response to this glorious gift is a life steeped in thankfulness. Every time you thank Me, you acknowledge that I am your Lord and Provider. This is the proper stance for a child of God: receiving with thanksgiving. Bring Me the sacrifice of gratitude, and watch to see how much I bless you.

*1 Peter 5:7; Ephesians 3:16–19;*
*Psalm 107:21–22*

# Wednesday

Wait with Me for a while. I have much to tell you. You are walking along the path I have chosen for you. It is both a privileged and a perilous way: experiencing My glorious Presence and heralding that reality to others. Sometimes you feel presumptuous to be carrying out such an assignment.

Do not worry about what other people think of you. The work I am doing in you is hidden at first. But eventually blossoms will burst forth, and abundant fruit will be borne. Stay on the path of Life with Me. Trust Me wholeheartedly, letting My Spirit fill you with Joy and Peace.

*1 Kings 8:23; Galatians 5:22–23*

## Thursday

Let thankfulness rule in your heart. As you thank Me for blessings in your life, a marvelous thing happens. It is as if *scales fall off your eyes*, enabling you to see more and more of My glorious riches. With your eyes thus opened, you can help yourself to whatever you need from My treasure house. Each time you receive one of My golden gifts, let your thankfulness sing out praises to My Name. "Hallelujahs" are the language of heaven, and they can become the language of your heart.

A life of praise and thankfulness becomes a life filled with miracles. Instead of trying to be in control, you focus on Me and what I am doing. This is the power of praise: centering your entire being in Me. This is how I created you to live, for I made you in My own image. Enjoy abundant life by overflowing with praise and thankfulness.

*Colossians 3:15; Acts 9:18;*
*Revelation 19:3–6; Psalm 100:4–5*

# Friday

Trust and thankfulness will get you safely through this day. Trust protects you from worrying and obsessing. Thankfulness keeps you from criticizing and complaining: those "sister sins" that so easily entangle you.

Keeping your eyes on Me is the same thing as trusting Me. It is a free choice that you must make thousands of times daily. The more you choose to trust Me, the easier it becomes. Thought patterns of trust become etched into your brain. Relegate troubles to the periphery of your mind, so that I can be central in your thoughts. Thus you focus on Me, entrusting your concerns into My care.

*Colossians 2:6–7; Psalm 141:8; I Peter 5:7*

# Saturday

Keep your focus on Me. I have gifted you with amazing freedom, including the ability to choose the focal point of your mind. Only the crown of My creation has such remarkable capability; this is a sign of being *made in My image.*

Let the goal of this day be to *bring every thought captive to Me.* Whenever your mind wanders, lasso those thoughts and bring them into My Presence. In My radiant Light, anxious thoughts shrink and shrivel away. Judgmental thoughts are unmasked as you bask in My unconditional Love. Confused ideas are untangled while you rest in the simplicity of My Peace. *I will guard you and keep you in constant Peace, as you focus your mind on Me.*

*Psalm 8:5; Genesis 1:26–27;
2 Corinthians 10:5; Isaiah 26:3 (AMP)*

# Week 3

Do not feel guilty about taking time to be still in My Presence. You are simply responding to the tugs of divinity within you. I made you in My image, and I hid heaven in your heart.

## Dear Jesus,

Being still in Your Presence is quite a challenge, partly because I have to fend off guilt feelings. It seems somehow selfish to spend so much time seeking Your Face. However, at a deeper level, it seems like the most important thing I do.

I yearn for more than this world can provide. I know heaven will satisfy all those longings perfectly. Yet my seeking heart looks to You even now for a taste of that eternal reality.

Beloved, you were not designed to find total satisfaction in this world, because you were crafted in My image. Heaven is your ultimate home, and I placed a bit of heavenly matter in your heart so you would seek Me. I delight in your seeking heart.

Refuse to feel guilty about something that brings Me such pleasure!

Much of this world's angst is actually a longing for the perfection of heaven. Blatant sin is often a misguided attempt to fill that emptiness. The god of this age has blinded the minds of unbelievers, so they search for heaven in hellish ways: excesses and perversions of every kind. However, great sinners can be transformed into exceptional Christians when they turn their passionate appetites toward Me. My Love and forgiveness satisfy soul-hunger as nothing else can.

Look to the LORD and his strength; seek his face always.
**Psalm 105:4**

The god of this age has blinded the minds of unbelievers,
so that they cannot see the light of the gospel of the
glory of Christ, who is the image of God.
**2 Corinthians 4:4**

Why spend money on what is not bread, and your labor
on what does not satisfy? Listen, listen to me and eat
what is good, and your soul will delight in the richest of fare.
**Isaiah 55:2**

*Sunday*

I am your Father-God. Listen to Me! Learn what it means to be a child of the everlasting King. Your richest duty is devotion to Me. This duty is such a joyous privilege that it feels like a luxury. You tend to feel guilty about pushing back the boundaries of your life to make space for time alone with Me. The world is waiting to squeeze you into its mold and to crowd out time devoted to Me. The ways of the world have also warped your conscience, which punishes you for doing the very thing that pleases Me most: seeking My Face. Listen to Me above the clamor of voices trying to distract you. Ask My Spirit to control your mind, for He and I work in perfect harmony. Be still and attentive in My Presence. *You are on holy ground.*

*Isaiah 9:6; Zechariah 9:9 (NKJV);*
*Romans 8:15–16; Exodus 3:5*

## Monday

Let My Love enfold you in the radiance of My Glory. Sit still in the Light of My Presence, and receive My Peace. These quiet moments with Me transcend time, accomplishing far more than you can imagine. Bring Me the sacrifice of your time, and watch to see how abundantly I bless you and your loved ones.

Through the intimacy of our relationship, you are being *transformed* from the inside out. As you keep your focus on Me, I form you into the one I desire you to be. Your part is to yield to My creative work in you, neither resisting it nor trying to speed it up. Enjoy the tempo of a God-breathed life by letting Me set the pace. Hold My hand in childlike trust, and the way before you will open up step by step.

*Hebrews 13:15; 2 Corinthians 3:18;*
*Psalm 73:23–24*

# Tuesday

I meet you in the stillness of your soul. It is there that I seek to commune with you. A person who is open to My Presence is exceedingly precious to Me. My eyes *search to and fro throughout the earth*, looking for one whose heart is seeking Me. I see you trying to find Me; our mutual search results in joyful fulfillment.

Stillness of soul is increasingly rare in this world addicted to speed and noise. I am pleased with your desire to create a quiet space where you and I can meet. Don't be discouraged by the difficulty of achieving this goal. I monitor all your efforts and am blessed by each of your attempts to seek My Face.

*Zechariah 2:13; 2 Chronicles 16:9 (NKJV);*
*Psalm 23:2–3 (NKJV)*

## Wednesday

Come away with Me for a while. The world, with its nonstop demands, can be put on hold. Most people put Me on hold, rationalizing that someday they will find time to focus on Me. But the longer people push Me into the background of their lives, the harder it is for them to find Me.

You live among people who glorify busyness; they have made time a tyrant that controls their lives. Even those who know Me as Savior tend to march to the tempo of the world. They have bought into the illusion that more is always better: more meetings, more programs, more activity.

I have called you to follow Me on a solitary path, making time alone with Me your highest priority and deepest Joy. It is a pathway largely unappreciated and often despised. However, *you have chosen the better thing, which will never be taken away from you.* Moreover, as you walk close to Me, I can bless others through you.

*Song of Songs 2:13; Luke 10:42*

# Thursday

Seek My Face, and you will find all that you have longed for. The deepest yearnings of your heart are for intimacy with Me. I know, because I designed you to desire Me. Do not feel guilty about taking time to be still in My Presence. You are simply responding to the tugs of divinity within you. I made you in My image, and I hid heaven in your heart. Your yearning for Me is a form of homesickness: longing for your true home in heaven.

Do not be afraid to be different from other people. The path I have called you to travel is exquisitely right for you. The more closely you follow My leading, the more fully I can develop your gifts. To follow Me wholeheartedly, you must relinquish your desire to please other people. However, your closeness to Me will bless others by enabling you to shine brightly in this dark world.

*Psalm 42:1–2; Psalm 34:5; Philippians 2:15*

# Friday

Trust Me enough to spend ample time with Me, pushing back the demands of the day. Refuse to feel guilty about something that is so pleasing to Me, the King of the universe. Because I am omnipotent, I am able to bend time and events in your favor. You will find that you can accomplish *more* in less time, after you have given yourself to Me in rich communion. Also, as you align yourself with My perspective, you can sort out what is important and what is not.

Don't fall into the trap of being constantly on the go. Many, many things people do in My Name have no value in My kingdom. To avoid doing meaningless works, stay in continual communication with Me. *I will instruct you and teach you in the way you should go; I will counsel you with My eye upon you.*

*Luke 10:41–42; Psalm 32:8 (NASB)*

## Saturday

Time with Me cannot be rushed. When you are in a hurry, your mind flitters back and forth between Me and the tasks ahead of you. Push back the demands pressing in on you; create a safe space around you, a haven in which you can rest with Me. I also desire this time of focused attention and I use it to bless you, strengthening and equipping you for the day ahead. Thus, spending time with Me is a wise investment.

Bring Me the sacrifice of your precious time. This creates sacred space around you—space permeated with My Presence and My Peace.

*Psalm 119:27; 2 Chronicles 16:9;*
*Hebrews 13:15 (NKJV)*

# Week 4

Instead of striving for a predictable, safe lifestyle, seek to know Me in greater depth and breadth. I want to make your life a glorious adventure, but you must stop clinging to old ways.

Dear Jesus,

You know how ambivalent my heart is. I long for the glorious adventure that a life abandoned to You can be. At the same time I cling to old ways, because change frightens me. I feel safest when my life is predictable and things seem to be under control. Help me break free and discover the adventures You have planned for me.

Beloved, the greatest adventure is knowing Me superabundantly: discovering how wide and long and high and deep is My Love for you. The power of My vast Love can feel overwhelming. That is why many people choose to limit their knowledge of Me, keeping Me at a safe distance. How that grieves Me! People settle for mediocrity because it feels more comfortable. However, they continue to battle fear. Only My Love is strong enough to break the hold that fear has on you. A predictable lifestyle may feel safer, but it can shield you from what you need most of all—Me!

When unexpected events shake up your routines, rejoice. This is exactly what you need to wake you up and point you toward Me. Recognize that you are on the threshold of a new adventure, and that I will be with you every step of the way. As we venture out together, cling tightly to My hand. The more you abandon yourself to Me, the more exuberantly you can experience My Love.

And I pray that you, being rooted and established in love,
may have power, together with all the saints, to grasp
how wide and long and high and deep is the love of Christ.
*Ephesians 3:17–18*

There is no fear in love. But perfect love drives out fear,
because fear has to do with punishment.
The one who fears is not made perfect in love.
*1 John 4:18*

My soul clings to you; your right hand upholds me.
*Psalm 63:8*

*Sunday*

D raw near to Me with a thankful heart, aware that your cup is overflowing with blessings. Gratitude enables you to perceive Me more clearly and to rejoice in our Love-relationship. *Nothing can separate you from My loving Presence!* That is the basis of your security. Whenever you start to feel anxious, remind yourself that your security rests in Me alone, and I am totally trustworthy.

You will never be in control of your life circumstances, but you can relax and trust in My control. Instead of striving for a predictable, safe lifestyle, seek to know Me in greater depth and breadth. I long to make your life a glorious adventure, but you must stop clinging to old ways. I am always doing something new within My beloved ones. Be on the lookout for all that I have prepared for you.

*Romans 8:38–39; Psalm 56:3–4; Isaiah 43:19*

## Monday

Be willing to go out on a limb with Me. If that is where I am leading you, it is the safest place to be. Your desire to live a risk-free life is a form of unbelief. Your longing to live close to Me is at odds with your attempts to minimize risk. You are approaching a crossroads in your journey. In order to follow Me wholeheartedly, you must relinquish your tendency to play it safe.

Let Me lead you step by step through this day. If your primary focus is on Me, you can walk along perilous paths without being afraid. Eventually, you will learn to relax and enjoy the adventure of our journey together. As long as you stay close to Me, My sovereign Presence protects you wherever you go.

*Psalm 23:4; Psalm 9:10; John 12:26*

## Tuesday

Give yourself fully to the adventure of today. Walk boldly along the path of Life, relying on your ever-present Companion. You have every reason to be confident, because My Presence accompanies you all the days of your life—and onward into eternity. Do not give in to fear or worry, those robbers of abundant living. Trust Me enough to face problems as they come, rather than trying to anticipate them. *Fix your eyes on Me, the Author and Perfecter of your faith,* and many difficulties on the road ahead will vanish before you reach them. Whenever you start to feel afraid, remember that *I am holding you by your right hand.* Nothing can separate you from My Presence!

**Hebrews 12:2; Isaiah 41:13**

# Wednesday

Worship Me by living close to Me. This was My original design for man, into whom *I breathed My very breath of Life*. This is My desire for you: that you stay near Me as you walk along your life-path. Each day is an important part of that journey. Although you may feel as if you are going nowhere in this world, your spiritual journey is another matter altogether, taking you along steep, treacherous paths of adventure. That is why *walking in the Light of My Presence* is essential to keep you from stumbling. By staying close to Me , you present yourself as a *living sacrifice*. Even the most routine part of your day can be *a spiritual act of worship, holy and pleasing to Me.*

*Genesis 2:7; Psalm 89:15; Romans 12:1–2*

*Thursday*

As you become increasingly aware of My Presence, you find it easier to discern the way you should go. This is one of the practical benefits of living close to Me. Instead of wondering about what is on the road ahead or worrying about what you should do if . . . or when . . . , you can concentrate on staying in communication with Me. When you actually arrive at a choice-point, I will show you which direction to go.

Many people are so preoccupied with future plans and decisions that they fail to see choices they need to make today. Without any conscious awareness, they make their habitual responses. People who live this way find a dullness creeping into their lives. They sleepwalk through their days, following well-worn paths of routine.

I, the Creator of the universe, am the most creative Being imaginable. I will not leave you circling in deeply rutted paths. Instead, I will lead you along fresh trails of adventure, revealing to you things you did not know. Stay in communication with Me. Follow My guiding Presence.

**Psalm 32:8; Genesis 1:1**

# *Friday*

Keep walking with Me along the path I have chosen for you. Your desire to live close to Me is a delight to My heart. I could instantly grant you the spiritual riches you desire, but that is not My way for you. Together we will forge a pathway up the high mountain. The journey is arduous at times, and you are weak. Someday you will dance lightfooted on the high peaks; but for now, your walk is often plodding and heavy. All I require of you is to take the next step, clinging to My hand for strength and direction. Though the path is difficult and the scenery dull at the moment, there are sparkling surprises just around the bend. Stay on the path I have selected for you. It is truly the *path of Life*.

**Psalm 37:23–24; Psalm 16:11 (NKJV)**

*Saturday*

I am leading you along the high road, but there are descents as well as ascents. In the distance you see snow-covered peaks glistening in brilliant sunlight. Your longing to reach those peaks is good, but you must not take shortcuts. Your assignment is to follow Me, allowing Me to direct your path. Let the heights beckon you onward, but stay close to Me.

Learn to trust Me when things go "wrong." Disruptions to your routine highlight your dependence on Me. Trusting acceptance of trials brings blessings that *far outweigh them all*. Walk hand in hand with Me through this day. I have lovingly planned every inch of the way. Trust does not falter when the path becomes rocky and steep. Breathe deep draughts of My Presence, and hold tightly to My hand. Together we can make it!

*John 21:19; 2 Corinthians 4:17;*
*Habakkuk 3:19*

# Week 5

My Power flows most freely into weak
ones aware of their need for Me.
Faltering steps of dependence are not lack
of faith; they are links to My Presence.

## Dear Jesus,

My journey is indeed one of faltering steps. Today I
feel as if it's a challenge just to take the next step. I find
it all too easy to be aware of my neediness. If I didn't
know You were with me, I would despair. I confess
that I sometimes get discouraged about my ongoing
weaknesses. I know that dependence on You brings
spiritual blessings, yet at times I feel trapped by my
limitations.

Beloved, awareness of your need for Me creates a
strong connection to My Presence. My Power
flows into you continually: It gives you strength
to take the next faltering step, strength to resist
discouragement and despair, strength to know Me in
intimate dependence. Only My Power can provide such
strength, enabling you to live abundantly in the midst
of your limitations. Your day-to-day perseverance, in

dependence on Me, is every bit as supernatural as an outright miracle.

Because you are My beloved child, I choose to bless you. However, I bless you in ways that are unique to your needs and My design for you. Your difficulties do not signify lack of faith or lack of blessing. They are means to help you stay on the path I have chosen for you. Though the way before you may be steep and rocky, it is nonetheless the path of Life. It is where you encounter My luminous Presence—radiating Peace that transcends your limitations.

Though the fig tree does not bud and there are no grapes on the vines, though the olive crop fails and the fields produce no food, though there are no sheep in the pen and no cattle in the stalls, yet I will rejoice in the LORD, I will be joyful in God my Savior. The sovereign LORD is my strength; he makes my feet like the feet of a deer, he enables me to go on the heights.
*Habakkuk 3:17–19*

To him who is able to keep you from falling and to present you before his glorious presence without fault and with great joy— to the only God our Savior be glory, majesty, power and authority, through Jesus Christ our Lord, before all ages, now and forevermore! Amen.
*Jude 1:24–25*

And the peace of God, which transcends all understanding, will guard your hearts and your minds in Christ Jesus.
*Philippians 4:7*

## Sunday

Come to Me for rest and refreshment. The journey has been too much for you, and you are bone-weary. Do not be ashamed of your exhaustion. Instead, see it as an opportunity for Me to take charge of your life.

Remember that *I can fit everything into a pattern for good*, including the things you wish were different. Start with where you are at this point in time and space, accepting that this is where I intend you to be. You will get through today one step, one moment at a time. Your main responsibility is to remain attentive to Me, letting Me guide you through the many choices along your pathway.

This sounds like an easy assignment, but it is not. Your desire to live in My Presence goes against the grain of "the world, the flesh, and the devil." Much of your weariness results from your constant battle against these opponents. However, you are on the path of My choosing, so do not give up! *Hope in Me, for you will again praise Me for the help of My Presence.*

**Romans 8:28 (AMP); Psalm 42:11 (NASB)**

# Monday

I am above all things: your problems, your pain, and the swirling events in this ever-changing world. When you behold My Face, you rise above circumstances and rest with Me in *heavenly realms*. This is the way of Peace, living in the Light of My Presence. I guarantee that you will always have problems in this life, but they must not become your focus. When you feel yourself sinking in the sea of circumstances, say *"Help me, Jesus!"* and I will draw you back to Me. If you have to say that thousands of times daily, don't be discouraged. I know your weakness, and I meet you in that very place.

**Ephesians 2:6; Matthew 14:28–32**

## Tuesday

Trust Me and don't be afraid, for I am your Strength and Song. Think what it means to have Me as your Strength. I spoke the universe into existence; My Power is absolutely unlimited! Human weakness, consecrated to Me, is like a magnet, drawing My Power into your neediness. However, fear can block the flow of My Strength into you. Instead of trying to fight your fears, concentrate on trusting Me. When you relate to Me in confident trust, there is no limit to how much I can strengthen you.

Remember that I am also your Song. I want you to share My Joy, living in conscious awareness of My Presence. Rejoice as we journey together toward heaven; join Me in singing My Song.

*Isaiah 12:2–3; Psalm 21:6*

## Wednesday

L ie down in green pastures of Peace. Learn to unwind whenever possible, resting in the Presence of your Shepherd. This electronic age keeps My children "wired" much of the time, too tense to find Me in the midst of their moments. I built into your very being the need for rest. How twisted the world has become when people feel guilty about meeting this basic need! How much time and energy they waste by being always on the go, rather than taking time to seek My direction for their lives.

I have called you to walk with Me down *paths of Peace*. I want you to blaze a trail for others who desire to live in My peaceful Presence. I have chosen you less for your strengths than for your weaknesses, which amplify your need for Me. Depend on Me more and more, and I will shower Peace on all your paths.

*Psalm 23:1–3; Genesis 2:2–3; Luke 1:79*

*Thursday*

Come to Me with empty hands and an open heart, ready to receive abundant blessings. I know the depth and breadth of your neediness. Your life-path has been difficult, draining you of strength. Come to Me for nurture. Let Me fill you up with My Presence: I in you, and you in Me.

My Power flows most freely into weak ones aware of their need for Me. Faltering steps of dependence are not lack of faith; they are links to My Presence.

*John 17:20–23; Isaiah 40:29–31*

## Friday

Be still in the Light of My Presence, while I communicate Love to you. There is no force in the universe as powerful as My Love. You are constantly aware of limitations: your own and others'. But there is no limit to My Love; it fills all of space, time, and eternity.

*Now you see through a glass, darkly, but someday you will see Me face to Face.* Then you will be able to experience fully *how wide and long and high and deep is My Love for you.* If you were to experience that now, you would be overwhelmed to the point of feeling crushed. But you have an eternity ahead of you, absolutely guaranteed, during which you can enjoy My Presence in unrestricted ecstasy. For now, the knowledge of My loving Presence is sufficient to carry you through each day.

*1 Corinthians 13:12 (KJV);*
*Ephesians 3:16–19*

## Saturday

Bring Me your weakness, and receive My Peace. Accept yourself and your circumstances just as they are, remembering that I am sovereign over everything. Do not wear yourself out with analyzing and planning. Instead, let thankfulness and trust be your guides through this day; they will keep you close to Me. As you live in the radiance of My Presence, My Peace shines upon you. You will cease to notice how weak or strong you feel, because you will be focusing on Me. The best way to get through this day is step by step with Me. Continue this intimate journey, trusting that the path you are following is headed for heaven.

*Psalm 29:11; Numbers 6:24–26; Psalm 13:5*

# Week 6

If you learn to trust Me—really trust Me—
with your whole being, then nothing can
separate you from My Peace. Everything
you endure can be put to good use by
allowing it to train you in trusting Me.
This is how you foil the works of evil,
growing in grace through the very adversity
that was meant to harm you.

Dear Jesus,

My deepest desire is to trust You with my whole
being, but trusting does not come easily to me. I have,
however, become more open to accepting adversity as
a gift from You. Sometimes I just want relief from my
difficulties. At other times I am able to receive them as
blessings. Help me to allow my problems to train me
in trusting You.

Beloved, it helps to have an eternal perspective.
If your life on earth were all there is, it might
be reasonable to run from adversity and seek a life of
pleasure. However, your earthly lifespan is miniscule,
compared with the Glory that awaits you in heaven. A

large part of learning to trust Me is viewing your life through this big-picture perspective.

Your openness to accepting adversity as blessing shows that you are indeed learning to trust Me more. Your anticipation of good outcomes in the midst of hard times is a profound form of trust.

Remember that the evil one attacks you continually with burning arrows of accusation. If you use your shield of faith skillfully, you can stop those missiles and extinguish their flames. Even if some of the arrows find their mark and wound you, do not despair. I am the Great Physician: My loving Presence can both heal your wounds and train you to trust Me more. When you are wounded, come close to Me and pay attention to My teaching. As you do so, your faith will be strengthened, enabling you to grow in grace and knowledge of Me—the Lord of Peace.

But as for you, you meant evil against me; but God meant it for good, in order to bring it about as it is this day, to save many people alive.
*Genesis 50:20 NKJV*

In addition to all this, take up the shield of faith, with which you can extinguish all the flaming arrows of the evil one.
*Ephesians 6:16*

But grow in the grace and knowledge of our Lord and Savior Jesus Christ. To him be glory both now and forever! Amen.
*2 Peter 3:18*

# Sunday

I want you to learn a new habit. Try saying, "I trust You, Jesus" in response to whatever happens to you. If there is time, think about who I am in all My Power and Glory; ponder also the depth and breadth of My Love for you.

This simple practice will help you see Me in every situation, acknowledging My sovereign control over the universe. When you view events from this perspective—through the Light of My universal Presence—fear loses its grip on you. Adverse circumstances become growth opportunities when you affirm your trust in Me no matter what. You receive blessings gratefully, realizing they flow directly from My hand of grace. Your continual assertion of trusting Me will strengthen our relationship and keep you close to Me.

*Psalm 63:2; Isaiah 40:10–11; Psalm 139:7–10*

## Monday

Learn to live above your circumstances. This requires focused time with Me, the *One who overcame the world*. Trouble and distress are woven into the very fabric of this perishing world. Only My Life in you can empower you to face this endless flow of problems with *good cheer*.

As you sit quietly in My Presence, I shine Peace into your troubled mind and heart. Little by little, you are freed from earthly shackles and lifted up above your circumstances. You gain My perspective on your life, enabling you to distinguish between what is important and what is not. Rest in My Presence, *receiving Joy that no one can take away from you*.

*John 16:33 (NKJV); John 16:22*

# Tuesday

It is impossible to praise or thank Me too much. As it is written, *I inhabit the praises of My people.* Sometimes your adoration is a spontaneous overflow of Joy, in response to radiant beauty or rich blessings. At other times your praise is more disciplined and measured—an act of your will. I dwell equally in both types of praise. Thankfulness, also, is a royal road to draw near Me. A thankful heart has plenty of room for Me.

When you thank Me for the many pleasures I provide, you affirm that I am God, from whom all blessings flow. When adversity strikes and you thank Me anyway, your trust in My sovereignty is a showpiece in invisible realms. Fill up the spare moments of your life with praise and thanksgiving. This joyous discipline will help you live in the intimacy of My Presence.

*Psalm 22:3 (KJV); Psalm 146:1–2;*
*1 Thessalonians 5:18*

## Wednesday

You are Mine for all time—and beyond time, into eternity. No power can deny you your inheritance in heaven. I want you to realize how utterly secure you are! Even if you falter as you journey through life, I will never let go of your hand.

Knowing that your future is absolutely assured can free you to live abundantly today. I have prepared this day for you with the most tender concern and attention to detail. Instead of approaching the day as a blank page that you need to fill up, try living it in a responsive mode: being on the lookout for all that I am doing. This sounds easy, but it requires a deep level of trust, based on the knowledge that *My way is perfect*.

*Psalm 37:23–24; Psalm 18:30*

## Thursday

You are feeling weighed down by a plethora of problems, both big and small. They seem to require more and more of your attention, but you must not give in to those demands. When the difficulties in your life feel as if they're closing in on you, break free by spending quality time with Me. You need to remember who I AM in all My Power and Glory. Then, humbly bring Me your prayers and petitions. Your problems will pale when you view them in the Light of My Presence. You can learn to *be joyful in Me, your Savior,* even in the midst of adverse circumstances. Rely on Me, *your Strength; I make your feet like the feet of a deer, enabling you to go on the heights.*

**Exodus 3:14; Habakkuk 3:17–19**

*Friday*

My Peace is like a shaft of golden Light shining on you continuously. During days of bright sunshine, it may blend in with your surroundings. On darker days, My Peace stands out in sharp contrast to your circumstances. See times of darkness as opportunities for My Light to shine in transcendent splendor. I am training you to practice Peace that overpowers darkness. Collaborate with Me in this training. *Do not grow weary and lose heart.*

*John 1:4–5 (AMP) ; Hebrews 12:3*

*Saturday*

I want to be Central in your entire being. When your focus is firmly on Me, My Peace displaces fears and worries. They will encircle you, seeking entrance, so you must stay alert. Let trust and thankfulness stand guard, turning back fear before it can gain a foothold. *There is no fear in My Love,* which shines on you continually. Sit quietly in My Love-Light, while I bless you with radiant Peace. Turn your whole being to trusting and loving Me.

*2 Thessalonians 3:16; 1 John 4:18*

# Week 7

By gazing at Me, you gain My perspective on your life. This time with Me is essential for untangling your thoughts and smoothing out the day before you.

## Dear Jesus,

You can easily read my thoughts, and You assess their condition with perfect accuracy. I wake up each morning with thought-fragments racing through my mind. It's hard to untangle my own thinking, because my mental capacity is so limited when I first awake. However, I can look to You, to do for me what I am unable to do for myself.

Beloved, even when your thoughts are scrambled, you can indeed look to Me for help. Many people stumble out of bed in the morning and head straight for the coffee pot. Though they are not yet thinking clearly, they are conscious enough to move toward something that will help untangle their thoughts. I perform a similar function for you, when your mind stumbles in My direction. Ask Me to help you think My thoughts and see things from My perspective. I created you in My image so that you would have this amazing capacity.

As you wait in My Presence, I not only unscramble your thinking, I also straighten your path through the day. I am sovereign over every aspect of your life, so opening up the way before you is no problem for Me. Some people think they don't have time to begin their day with Me. They don't realize how much I can facilitate their activities—removing obstacles, giving insights that save time, and so on. When you spend precious time with Me, I compensate you generously: smoothing out the circumstances of your day.

O LORD, you have searched me and you know me.
You know when I sit and when I rise;
you perceive my thoughts from afar.
*Psalm 139:1–2*

So God created man in his own image, in the image
of God he created him; male and female he created them.
*Genesis 1:27*

We wait in hope for the LORD; he is our help and our shield.
In him our hearts rejoice, for we trust in his holy name.
May your unfailing love rest upon us, O LORD,
even as we put our hope in you.
*Psalm 33:20–22*

Sunday

*S*eek My Face at the beginning of your day. This practice enables you to "put Me on" and "wear Me" throughout the day. Most people put on clothes soon after arising from bed. Similarly, the sooner you "put Me on" by communicating with Me, the better prepared you are for whatever comes your way.

To "wear Me" is essentially to have My mind: to think My thoughts. Ask the Holy Spirit to control your thinking; be transformed by this renewal within you. Thus you are well equipped to face whatever people and situations I bring your way. Clothing your mind in Me is your best preparation for each day. This discipline brings Joy and Peace to you and those around you.

*Psalm 27:8 (NKJV); Romans 13:14;*
*Colossians 3:12*

## Monday

Try to view each day as an adventure, carefully planned out by your Guide. Instead of staring into the day that is ahead of you, attempting to program it according to your will, be attentive to Me and to all I have prepared for you. Thank Me for this day of life, recognizing that it is a precious, unrepeatable gift. Trust that I am with you each moment, whether you sense My Presence or not. A thankful, trusting attitude helps you to see events in your life from My perspective.

A life lived close to Me will never be dull or predictable. Expect each day to contain surprises! Resist your tendency to search for the easiest route through the day. Be willing to follow wherever I lead. No matter how steep or treacherous the path before you, the safest place to be is by My side.

*Psalm 118:24; 1 Peter 2:21*

*Tuesday*

Relax in My healing Presence. As you spend time with Me, your thoughts tend to jump ahead to today's plans and problems. Bring your mind back to Me for refreshment and renewal. Let the Light of My Presence soak into you, as you focus your thoughts on Me. Thus I equip you to face whatever the day brings. This sacrifice of time pleases Me and strengthens you. Do not skimp on our time together. Resist the clamor of tasks waiting to be done. *You have chosen what is better, and it will not be taken away from you.*

*Psalm 105:4; Luke 10:39–42*

# Wednesday

I am training you in steadiness. Too many things interrupt your awareness of Me. I know that you live in a world of sight and sound, but you must not be a slave to those stimuli. Awareness of Me can continue in all circumstances, no matter what happens. This is the steadiness I desire for you.

Don't let unexpected events throw you off course. Rather, respond calmly and confidently, remembering that I am with you. As soon as something grabs your attention, talk with Me about it. Thus I share your joys and your problems; I help you cope with whatever is before you. This is how I live in you and work through you. This is the way of Peace.

**Psalm 112:7; Isaiah 41:10 (NKJV)**

# Thursday

Come to Me with a thankful heart, so that you can enjoy My Presence. This is the day that I have made. I want you to rejoice *today*, refusing to worry about tomorrow. Search for all that I have prepared for you, anticipating abundant blessings and accepting difficulties as they come. I can weave miracles into the most mundane day if you keep your focus on Me.

Come to Me with all your needs, knowing that *My glorious riches* are a more-than-adequate supply. Stay in continual communication with Me, so that you can live above your circumstances even while you are in the midst of them. *Present your requests to Me with thanksgiving, and My Peace, which surpasses all comprehension, will guard your heart and mind.*

Psalm 118:24; Philippians 4:19, 6–7 (NASB)

# Friday

Let Me prepare you for the day that stretches out
before you. I know exactly what this day will
contain, whereas you have only vague ideas about it. You
would like to see a map, showing all the twists and turns
of your journey. You'd feel more prepared if you could
somehow visualize what is on the road ahead. However,
there is a better way to be prepared for *whatever* you will
encounter today: Spend quality time with Me.

I will not show you what is on the road ahead, but
I will thoroughly equip you for the journey. My living
Presence is your Companion each step of the way. Stay
in continual communication with Me, whispering My
Name whenever you need to redirect your thoughts.
Thus, you can walk through this day with your focus on
Me. My abiding Presence is the best road map available.

*Exodus 33:14; John 15:4–7*

## Saturday

Every time you affirm your trust in Me, you put a coin into My treasury. Thus you build up equity in preparation for days of trouble. I keep safely in My heart all trust invested in Me, with interest compounded continuously. The more you trust Me, the more I empower you to do so.

Practice trusting Me during quiet days, when nothing much seems to be happening. Then when storms come, your trust balance will be sufficient to see you through. *Store up for yourself treasure in heaven,* through placing your trust in Me. This practice will keep you in My Peace.

*Psalm 56:3–4; Matthew 6:20-21*

# Week 8

I am always before you, beckoning you on—one step at a time. Neither height nor depth, nor anything else in all creation, can separate you from My loving Presence.

Dear Jesus,

I want to live my life focused on Your Presence in the present. I believe You are always before me, leading and encouraging me, but I need to live out of that reality moment by moment. My mind tends to leap over the present moment to the next task, ignoring the one that is before me and the One who is before me. During rare times when I am able to stay focused on You, my work is infused with Your Presence. It is no longer laborious but delightful: more like play than work.

Beloved, living in collaboration with Me can be a foretaste of heaven. It is wonderful, though not easy: It requires a level of spiritual and mental concentration that is extremely challenging. In the Psalms, David wrote about this collaborative way of living, declaring that he had set Me always before him.

As a shepherd, he had plenty of time to seek My Face and enjoy My Presence. He discovered the beauty of days lived with Me always before him—and beside him. I am training you to live this way too. This endeavor requires more persistent effort than anything else you have attempted. Yet, rather than detracting from your other activities, it fills them with vibrant Life.

Whatever you do, do it for Me—with Me, through Me, in Me. Even menial tasks glow with the Joy of My Presence when you do them for Me. Ultimately, nothing will be able to separate you from Me. So this you-and-I-together venture can continue throughout eternity.

For I am convinced that neither death nor life, neither angels nor demons, neither the present nor the future, nor any powers, neither height nor depth, nor anything else in all creation, will be able to separate us from the love of God that is in Christ Jesus our Lord.

*Romans 8:38–39*

I have set the LORD always before me.
Because he is at my right hand, I will not be shaken.

*Psalm 16:8*

And whatever you do, do it heartily, as to the Lord and not to men, knowing that from the Lord you will receive the reward of the inheritance; for you serve the Lord Christ.

*Colossians 3:23-24 NKJV*

# Sunday

There is a mighty battle going on for control of your mind. Heaven and earth intersect in your mind; the tugs of both spheres influence your thinking. I created you with the capacity to experience foretastes of heaven. When you shut out the world and focus on My Presence, you can enjoy sitting with Me *in heavenly realms*. This is an incredible privilege reserved for precious ones who belong to Me and seek My Face. Your greatest strength is your desire to spend time communing with Me. As you concentrate on Me, *My Spirit fills your mind with Life and Peace*.

The world exerts a downward pull on your thoughts. Media bombard you with greed, lust, and cynicism. When you face these things, pray for protection and discernment. Stay in continual communication with Me whenever you walk through the wastelands of this world. Refuse to worry, because this form of worldliness will weigh you down. Stay alert, recognizing the battle being waged against your mind. Look forward to an eternity of strife-free living, reserved for you in heaven.

*Ephesians 2:6; Romans 8:6; 1 John 2:15–17*

## Monday

I am the eternal *I AM*; I always have been, and I always will be. In My Presence you experience Love and Light, Peace and Joy. I am intimately involved in all your moments, and I am training you to be aware of Me at all times. Your assignment is to collaborate with Me in this training process.

I have taken up residence within you; I am central in your innermost being. Your mind goes off in tangents from its holy Center, time after time. Do not be alarmed by your inability to remain focused on Me. Simply bring your thoughts gently back to Me each time they wander. The quickest way to redirect your mind to me is to whisper My Name.

*Exodus 3:14; 1 Corinthians 3:16;*
*Psalm 25:14–15*

## Tuesday

*I am renewing your mind.* When your thoughts flow freely, they tend to move toward problems. Your focus gets snagged on a given problem, circling round and round it in attempts to gain mastery. Your energy is drained away from other matters through this negative focus. Worst of all, you lose sight of Me.

A renewed mind is Presence-focused. Train your mind to seek Me in every moment, every situation. Sometimes you can find Me in your surroundings: a lilting birdsong, a loved one's smile, golden sunlight. At other times, you must draw inward to find Me. I am always present in your spirit. *Seek My Face,* speak to Me, and I will light up your mind.

**Romans 12:2; Psalm 105:4**

*Wednesday*

*I am with you.* These four words are like a safety net, protecting you from falling into despair. Because you are human, you will always have ups and downs in your life experience. But the promise of My Presence limits how far down you can go. Sometimes you may feel as if you are in a free fall, when people or things you had counted on let you down. Yet as soon as you remember that *I am with you,* your perspective changes radically. Instead of bemoaning your circumstances, you can look to Me for help. You recall that not only am I with you, *I am holding you by your right hand. I guide you with My counsel, and afterward I will take you into Glory.* This is exactly the perspective you need: the reassurance of My Presence, and the glorious hope of heaven.

**Zephaniah 3:17; Psalm 73:23–26**

## Thursday

*I am with you always.* These were the last words I spoke before ascending into heaven. I continue to proclaim this promise to all who will listen. People respond to My continual Presence in various ways. Most Christians accept this teaching as truth but ignore it in their daily living. Some ill-taught or wounded believers fear (and may even resent) My awareness of all they do, say, and think. A few people center their lives around this glorious promise and find themselves blessed beyond all expectations.

When My Presence is the focal point of your consciousness, all the pieces of your life fall into place. As you gaze at Me through the eyes of your heart, you can see the world around you from My perspective. The fact that *I am with you* makes every moment of your life meaningful.

*Matthew 28:20; Psalm 139:1–4*

*Friday*

Rest in My Presence, allowing Me to take charge of this day. Do not bolt into the day like a racehorse suddenly released. Instead, walk purposefully with Me, letting Me direct your course one step at a time. Thank Me for each blessing along the way; this brings Joy to both you and Me. A grateful heart protects you from negative thinking. Thankfulness enables you to see the abundance I shower upon you daily. Your prayers and petitions are winged into heaven's throne room when they are permeated with thanksgiving. *In everything give thanks, for this is My will for you.*

Colossians 4:2;
1 Thessalonians 5:18 (NASB)

## Saturday

Refresh yourself in the Peace of My Presence. This Peace can be your portion at all times and in all circumstances. Learn to *hide in the secret of My Presence,* even as you carry out your duties in the world. I am both with you and within you. I go before you to open up the way, and I also walk alongside you. There could never be another companion as devoted as I am.

Because I am your constant Companion, there should be a lightness to your step that is observable to others. Do not be weighed down with problems and unresolved issues, for I am your burden-bearer. In the world you have trials and distress, but don't let them get you down. *I have conquered the world and deprived it of power to harm you.* In Me you may have confident Peace.

*Psalm 31:19–20 (NASB); John 16:33 (AMP)*

# Week 9

Nothing is wasted when you walk
close to Me. Even your mistakes can be
recycled into something good, through
My transforming grace.

## Dear Jesus,

I desperately want to believe that my mistakes can
somehow be used for good in Your kingdom. The truth
is, I hate making mistakes! This attitude can easily
translate into hating myself for having messed up. When
I let my mind run freely at such a time, I find myself
fantasizing about *what might have been*—if only I had
acted or chosen differently. I definitely need a strong
dose of Your transforming grace!

Beloved, the best strategy for accepting yourself,
even when you make mistakes, is living close to Me.
This nearness helps you see things from My perspective.
You tend to view yourself as someone who should be
almost perfect, making very few errors. My perspective
is quite different: I see you as My beloved child—weak
in many ways, prone to wandering from Me. However,

your weakness and waywardness cannot diminish My constant Love for you. Moreover, My infinite wisdom enables Me to take your errors and weave them into an intricate work that is good.

You need to accept not only yourself but also the choices you have made. Fantasizing about having done things differently is a time-wasting trap. It is impossible to live close to Me while you're indulging in such unreality. The more you fantasize, the further from Me you wander. When you realize this has happened, turn around and run back to Me! Take time to talk with Me and relax in My Presence. Your perfectionist tendencies will dissolve as you soak in My transforming grace

As a father has compassion on his children, so the LORD
has compassion on those who fear him; for he knows how
we are formed, he remembers that we are dust.
*Psalm 103:13–14*

May your unfailing love be my comfort,
according to your promise to your servant.
*Psalm 119:76*

In him we have redemption through his blood, the forgiveness
of sins, in accordance with the riches of God's grace that he
lavished on us with all wisdom and understanding.
*Ephesians 1:7–8*

*Sunday*

Don't be so hard on yourself. I can bring good even out of your mistakes. Your finite mind tends to look backward, longing to undo decisions you have come to regret. This is a waste of time and energy, leading only to frustration. Instead of floundering in the past, release your mistakes to Me. Look to Me in trust, anticipating that My infinite creativity can weave both good choices and bad into a lovely design.

Because you are human, you will continue to make mistakes. Thinking that you should live an error-free life is symptomatic of pride. Your failures can be a source of blessing, humbling you and giving you empathy for other people in their weaknesses. Best of all, failure highlights your dependence on Me. I am able to bring beauty out of the morass of your mistakes. Trust Me, and watch to see what I will do.

*Romans 8:28; Micah 7:7*

## Monday

Trust Me in every detail of your life. Nothing is random in My kingdom. *Everything that happens fits into a pattern for good, to those who love Me.* Instead of trying to analyze the intricacies of the pattern, focus your energy on trusting Me and thanking Me at all times. Nothing is wasted when you walk close to Me. Even your mistakes and sins can be recycled into something good, through My transforming grace.

While you were still living in darkness, I began to shine the Light of My Presence into your sin-stained life. Finally, *I lifted you up out of the mire into My marvelous Light.* Having sacrificed My very Life for you, I can be trusted in every facet of your life.

*Jeremiah 17:7; Romans 8:28 (AMP); Psalm 40:2;
1 Peter 2:9 (NKJV)*

# Tuesday

Strive to trust Me in more and more areas of your life. Anything that tends to make you anxious is a growth opportunity. Instead of running away from these challenges, embrace them, eager to gain all the blessings I have hidden in the difficulties. If you believe that I am sovereign over every aspect of your life, it is possible to trust Me in all situations. Don't waste energy regretting the way things are or thinking about what might have been. Start at the present moment—accepting things exactly as they are—and search for My way in the midst of those circumstances.

Trust is like a staff you can lean on, as you journey uphill with Me. If you are trusting in Me consistently, the staff will bear as much of your weight as needed. *Lean on, trust, and be confident in Me with all your heart and mind.*

**Psalm 52:8; Proverbs 3:5–6 (AMP)**

# Wednesday

Rest in Me, My child. This time devoted to Me is meant to be peaceful, not stressful. You don't have to perform in order to receive My Love. I have boundless, unconditional Love for you. How it grieves Me to see My children working for Love: trying harder and harder, yet never feeling good enough to be loved.

Be careful that your devotion to Me does not become another form of works. I want you to come into My Presence joyfully and confidently. You have nothing to fear, for you wear My own righteousness. Gaze into My eyes, and you will see no condemnation, only Love and delight in the one I see. Be blessed as *My Face shines radiantly upon you, giving you Peace.*

*John 15:13; Zephaniah 3:17;*
*Numbers 6:25–26*

## Thursday

I am your best Friend, as well as your King. Walk hand in hand with Me through your life. Together we will face whatever each day brings: pleasures, hardships, adventures, disappointments. Nothing is wasted when it is shared with Me. *I can bring beauty out of the ashes* of lost dreams. I can glean Joy out of sorrow, Peace out of adversity. Only a Friend who is also the King of kings could accomplish this divine alchemy. There is no other like Me!

The friendship I offer you is practical and down-to-earth, yet it is saturated with heavenly Glory. Living in My Presence means living in two realms simultaneously: the visible world and unseen, eternal reality. I have equipped you to stay conscious of Me while walking along dusty, earthbound paths.

*John 15:13–15; Isaiah 61:3;*
*2 Corinthians 6:10*

*Friday*

You can achieve the victorious life through living in deep dependence on Me. People usually associate victory with success: not falling or stumbling, not making mistakes. But those who are successful in their own strength tend to go their own way, forgetting about Me. It is through problems and failure, weakness and neediness that you learn to rely on Me.

True dependence is not simply asking Me to bless what you have decided to do. It is coming to Me with an open mind and heart, inviting Me to plant My desires within you. I may infuse within you a dream that seems far beyond your reach. You know that in yourself you cannot achieve such a goal. Thus begins your journey of profound reliance on Me. It is a faith-walk, taken one step at a time, leaning on Me as much as you need. This is not a path of continual success but of multiple failures. However, each failure is followed by a growth spurt, nourished by increased reliance on Me. Enjoy the blessedness of a victorious life, through deepening your dependence on Me.

*Psalm 34:17–18; 2 Corinthians 5:7 (NKJV)*

## Saturday

Thank Me for the glorious gift of My Spirit. This is like priming the pump of a well. As you bring Me the sacrifice of thanksgiving, regardless of your feelings, My Spirit is able to work more freely within you. This produces more thankfulness and more freedom, until you are overflowing with gratitude.

I shower blessings on you daily, but sometimes you don't perceive them. When your mind is stuck on a negative focus, you see neither Me nor My gifts. In faith, thank Me for whatever is preoccupying your mind. This will clear the blockage so that you can find Me.

*2 Corinthians 5:5; 2 Corinthians 3:17;*
*Psalm 50:14*

# Week 10

I comprehend you in all your complexity;
no detail of your life is hidden from Me.
I view you through eyes of grace, so don't
be afraid of My intimate awareness.

## Dear Jesus,

It is totally amazing that You understand me—all
of me—with absolute accuracy. That could also be
terrifying, if You saw me through eyes of law rather than
grace. Unfortunately, I often view myself legalistically:
evaluating how well I'm performing. I realize how
silly that is, because my performance will always be
insufficient to meet Your holy standard. That's why I
desperately need Your grace! Please help me see myself,
as well as others, through eyes of grace.

Beloved, come to Me and receive My unfailing
Love. You are troubled by fear of failure, but
My Love for you will never fail. Let Me describe
what I see, as I view you through eyes of grace.
You look regal, for I have clothed you in My royal
righteousness. You also look radiant, especially when

you are gazing at Me. You are lovely as you reflect My Glory back to Me. In fact, you delight Me so much that I rejoice over you with shouts of Joy! This is how you appear through My vision of grace.

Because I am infinite, I can see you simultaneously as you are now and as you will be in heaven. The present view helps Me work with you on things you need to change. The heavenly vision enables Me to love you with perfect, everlasting Love.

The best way to see through eyes of grace is to look through the lens of My unfailing Love. As you persevere in this practice, you will gradually find it easier to extend grace both to yourself and to others.

How priceless is your unfailing love!
Both high and low among men
find refuge in the shadow of your wings.
*Psalm 36:7*

I sought the LORD, and he answered me; he delivered me
from all my fears. Those who look to him are radiant;
their faces are never covered with shame.
*Psalm 34:4–5*

The LORD your God is in your midst,...
He will exult over you with joy,...
He will rejoice over you with shouts of joy.
*Zephaniah 3:17 NASB*

*Sunday*

Relax in My peaceful Presence. Do not bring performance pressures into our sacred space of communion. When you are with someone you trust completely, you feel free to be yourself. This is one of the joys of true friendship. Though I am *Lord of lords and King of kings,* I also desire to be your intimate Friend. When you are tense or pretentious in our relationship, I feel hurt. I know the worst about you, but I also see the best in you. I long for you to trust Me enough to be fully yourself with Me. When you are real with Me, I am able to bring out the best in you: the very gifts I have planted in your soul. Relax, and enjoy our friendship.

*Revelation 17:14; John 15:13–15*

*Monday*

Stop judging and evaluating yourself, for this is not your role. Above all, stop comparing yourself with other people. This produces feelings of pride or inferiority; sometimes, a mixture of both. I lead each of My children along a path that is uniquely tailor-made for him or her. Comparing is not only wrong; it is also meaningless.

Don't look for affirmation in the wrong places: your own evaluations, or those of other people. The only source of real affirmation is My unconditional Love. Many believers perceive Me as an unpleasable Judge, angrily searching out their faults and failures. Nothing could be farther from the truth! I died for your sins, so that I might *clothe you in My garments of salvation.* This is how I see you: *radiant in My robe of righteousness.* When I discipline you, it is never in anger or disgust; it is to prepare you for face-to-Face fellowship with Me throughout all eternity. Immerse yourself in My loving Presence. Be receptive to My affirmation, which flows continually from the throne of grace.

*Luke 6:37; Isaiah 61:10 (NASB); Proverbs 3:11–12*

*Tuesday*

Do not hesitate to receive Joy from Me, for I bestow it on you abundantly. The more you rest in My Presence, the more freely My blessings flow into you. In the Light of My Love, you are gradually *transformed from glory to glory*. It is through spending time with Me that you realize *how wide and long and high and deep is My Love for you*.

Sometimes the relationship I offer you seems too good to be true. I pour My very Life into you, and all you have to do is receive Me. In a world characterized by working and taking, the admonition to rest and receive seems too easy. There is an intricate connection between receiving and believing: As you trust Me more and more, you are able to receive Me and My blessings abundantly. *Be still, and know that I am God.*

*2 Corinthians 3:18 (NASB);*
*Ephesians 3:17–19; Psalm 46:10*

## Wednesday

Come to Me for understanding, since I know you far better than you know yourself. I comprehend you in all your complexity; *no detail of your life is hidden from Me.* I view you through eyes of grace, so don't be afraid of My intimate awareness. Allow the Light of My healing Presence to shine into the deepest recesses of your being–cleansing, healing, refreshing, and renewing you. Trust Me enough to accept the full forgiveness that I offer you continually. This great gift, which cost Me My Life, is yours for all eternity. Forgiveness is at the very core of My abiding Presence. *I will never leave you or forsake you.*

When no one else seems to understand you, simply draw closer to Me. Rejoice in the One who understands you completely and loves you perfectly. As I fill you with My Love, you become a reservoir of love, overflowing into the lives of other people.

*Psalm 139:1–4; 2 Corinthians 1:21–22;*
*Joshua 1:5*

# Thursday

Let Me fill you with my Love, Joy, and Peace. These are Glory-gifts, flowing from my living Presence. Though you are an *earthen vessel*, I designed you to be filled with heavenly contents. Your weakness is not a deterrent to being filled with My Spirit; on the contrary, it provides an opportunity for My Power to shine forth more brightly.

As you go through this day, trust Me to provide the strength that you need moment by moment. Don't waste energy wondering whether you are adequate for today's journey. My Spirit within you is more than sufficient to handle whatever this day may bring. That is the basis for your confidence! *In quietness* (spending time alone with Me) *and confident trust* (relying on My sufficiency) *is your strength.*

2 Corinthians 4:7 (NASB); Isaiah 30:15

## Friday

**B**ask in the luxury of being fully understood and unconditionally loved. Dare to see yourself as I see you: radiant in My righteousness, cleansed by My blood. I view you as the one I created you to be, the one you will be in actuality when heaven becomes your home. It is My Life within you that is changing you *from glory to glory*. Rejoice in this mysterious miracle! Thank Me continually for the amazing gift of My Spirit within you.

Try to depend on the help of the Spirit as you go through this day of life. Pause briefly from time to time so you can consult with this Holy One inside you. He will not force you to do His bidding, but He will guide you as you give Him space in your life. Walk along this wondrous way of collaboration with My Spirit.

*Psalm 34:5; 2 Corinthians 5:21;*
*2 Corinthians 3:18 (NKJV); Galatians 5:25*

*Saturday*

I am pleased with you, My child. Allow yourself to become fully aware of My pleasure shining upon you. You don't have to perform well in order to receive My Love. In fact, a performance focus will pull you away from Me, toward some sort of Pharisaism. This can be a subtle form of idolatry: worshiping your own good works. It can also be a source of deep discouragement when your works don't measure up to your expectations.

Shift your focus from your performance to My radiant Presence. The Light of My Love shines on you continually, regardless of your feelings or behavior. Your responsibility is to be receptive to this unconditional Love. Thankfulness and trust are your primary receptors. Thank Me for everything; *trust in Me at all times*. These simple disciplines will keep you open to My loving Presence.

*Ephesians 2:8–9; Ephesians 3:16–19;*
*Psalm 62:8*

# Week 11

What I search for in My children is an awakened soul that thrills to the Joy of My Presence! I created mankind to glorify and enjoy Me forever. I provide the Joy; your part is to glorify Me by living close to Me.

## Dear Jesus,

I long to have a fully awakened soul! I've discovered that nothing is more satisfying than the Joy of your Presence. However, I'm often subject to a slumbering soul: taking for granted my life with all its blessings, being overly focused on negative things, buying into the world's version of the good life. Help me break free from these worldly weights, so my soul can soar in the heights with You.

Beloved, the fact that you yearn for an awakened soul is itself a source of pleasure to Me. Many of My children view devotion to Me as a duty, and they look elsewhere for their pleasures. They fail to understand that the Joy of My Presence outshines even the most delightful earthly joy. Of course, it is not an either/or situation. You don't have to choose between enjoying Me or enjoying the many good gifts I provide. It is simply a matter of priorities: I want you to treasure Me above all else. Actually, the more fully you enjoy Me, the more capacity you have to appreciate the blessings I shower upon you. When you make Me your ultimate Pleasure, you glorify Me by desiring closeness with Me. As you delight in Me, I am free to bless you with many things that please you. If you keep Me first in your life, My good gifts will not become idols. Delight yourself in Me, and I will give you the desires and secret petitions of your heart.

For the eyes of the LORD range throughout the earth
to strengthen those whose hearts are fully committed to him.
*2 Chronicles 16:9*

You have made known to me the paths of life;
you will fill me with joy in your presence.
*Acts 2:28*

Every good and perfect gift is from above,
coming down from the Father of the heavenly lights,
who does not change like shifting shadows.
*James 1:17*

Delight yourself also in the LORD, and He will give you the desires
and secret petitions of your heart.
*Psalm 37:4 AMP*

## *Sunday*

I *am the resurrection and the Life*; all lasting Life emanates from Me. People search for life in many wrong ways: chasing after fleeting pleasures, accumulating possessions and wealth, trying to deny the inevitable effects of aging. Meanwhile, I freely offer abundant Life to everyone who turns toward Me. As you *come to Me and take My yoke upon you*, I fill you with My very Life. This is how I choose to live in the world and accomplish My purposes. This is also how I bless you with *Joy unspeakable and full of Glory*. The Joy is Mine, and the Glory is Mine; but I bestow them on you as you live in My Presence, inviting Me to live fully in you.

*John 11:25; Matthew 11:28–29;*
*1 Peter 1:8–9 (KJV)*

*Monday*

Save your best striving for seeking My Face. I am constantly communicating with you. To find Me and hear My voice, you must seek Me above all else. Anything that you desire more than Me becomes an idol. When you are determined to get your own way, you blot Me out of your consciousness. Instead of single-mindedly pursuing some goal, talk with Me about it. Let the Light of My Presence shine on this pursuit so that you can see it from My perspective. If the goal fits into My plans for you, I will help you reach it. If it is contrary to My will for you, I will gradually change the desire of your heart. *Seek Me first* and foremost; then the rest of your life will fall into place, piece by piece.

*1 Chronicles 16:11; Matthew 6:33*

## Tuesday

I am a God who gives and gives and gives. When I died for you on the cross, I held back nothing; I poured out My Life *like a drink offering*. Because giving is inherent in My nature, I search for people who are able to receive in full measure. To increase your intimacy with Me, the two traits you need the most are receptivity and attentiveness. Receptivity is opening up your innermost being to be filled with My abundant riches. Attentiveness is directing your gaze to Me: searching for Me in all your moments. It *is* possible to *stay your mind on Me,* as the prophet Isaiah wrote. Through such attentiveness you receive a glorious gift: My perfect Peace.

*Philippians 2:17; Mark 10:15;*
*Isaiah 26:3 (NKJV)*

## Wednesday

Let thankfulness temper all your thoughts. A thankful mind-set keeps you in touch with Me. I hate it when My children grumble, casually despising My sovereignty. Thankfulness is a safeguard against this deadly sin. Furthermore, a grateful attitude becomes a grid through which you perceive life. Gratitude enables you to see the Light of My Presence shining on all your circumstances. Cultivate a thankful heart, for this glorifies Me and fills you with Joy.

*1 Corinthians 10:10; Hebrews 12:28–29*

# Thursday

Listen to the love song that I am continually singing to you. *I take great delight in you . . . I rejoice over you with singing.* The voices of the world are a cacophony of chaos, pulling you this way and that. Don't listen to those voices; challenge them with My Word. Learn to take minibreaks from the world, finding a place to be still in My Presence and listen to My voice.

There is immense hidden treasure to be found through listening to Me. Though I pour out blessings upon you always, some of My richest blessings have to be actively sought. I love to reveal Myself to you, and your seeking heart opens you up to receive more of My disclosure. *Ask and it will be given to you; seek and you will find; knock and the door will be opened to you.*

*Zephaniah 3:17; Matthew 7:7*

*Friday*

Bring Me the sacrifice of thanksgiving. Take nothing for granted, not even the rising of the sun. Before Satan tempted Eve in the Garden of Eden, thankfulness was as natural as breathing. Satan's temptation involved pointing Eve to the one thing that was forbidden her. The garden was filled with luscious, desirable fruits, but Eve focused on the one fruit she couldn't have rather than being thankful for the many good things freely available. This negative focus darkened her mind, and she succumbed to temptation.

When you focus on what you don't have or on situations that displease you, your mind also becomes darkened. You take for granted life, salvation, sunshine, flowers, and countless other gifts from Me. You look for what is wrong and refuse to enjoy life until that is "fixed."

When you approach Me with thanksgiving, the Light of My Presence pours into you, transforming you through and through. *Walk in the Light* with Me by practicing the discipline of thanksgiving.

*Psalm 116:17 (NKJV); Genesis 3:2–6; 1 John 1:7*

*Saturday*

Be still in My Presence, even though countless tasks clamor for your attention. Nothing is as important as spending time with Me. While you wait in My Presence, I do My best work within you: *transforming you by the renewing of your mind.* If you skimp on this time with Me, you may plunge headlong into the wrong activities, missing the richness of what I have planned for you.

Do not seek Me primarily for what I can give you. Remember that I, the Giver, am infinitely greater than any gift I might impart to you. Though I delight in blessing My children, I am deeply grieved when My blessings become idols in their hearts. Anything can be an idol if it distracts you from Me as your *First Love.* When I am the ultimate Desire of your heart, you are safe from the danger of idolatry. As you wait in My Presence, enjoy the greatest gift of all: *Christ in you, the hope of Glory!*

*Romans 12:2; Revelation 2:4;*
*Colossians 1:27*

# Week 12

Waiting, trusting, and hoping are intricately connected: like golden strands interwoven to form a strong chain. Trusting is the central strand, because it is the response from My children that I desire the most.

*Dear Jesus,*

Often I feel as if waiting is what I do most of the time. I admit that it is difficult for me to wait: I prefer to make things happen myself, without delay. Hoping feels very similar to waiting; it is all about future things that are beyond my control. However, I have found that when I'm actively trusting You, waiting and hoping flow naturally out of my closeness with You.

Beloved, trusting Me is crucial, and it gives meaning to your waiting and hoping. Without trust, your connection with Me quickly deteriorates. That's why the Bible contains so many commands to trust Me. As you affirm your faith in Me, I empower you to wait with positive expectations. Waiting on Me is actually a great privilege, full of promise and blessing. Waiting on royalty has always been considered a high position, because it involves nearness to the royal persons. Ladies-in-waiting may perform humble services, such as helping people dress; yet these helpers are highly esteemed, even though they serve sinful, mortal royals. How much more should you treasure the privilege of serving Me—the King of eternity, immortal, invisible, the only God!

Hoping can be a joyful occupation, because it connects you to your promised inheritance in heaven. Such hope provides a rock-solid foundation in the present, helping you face the daily struggles of living in a broken world. Hope also connects you with Me, for I am the God of hope. My death on the cross opened the way for you to join My royal family and live with Me forever.

Trust in him at all times, O people; pour out your hearts
to him, for God is our refuge.
*Psalm 62:8*

Now to the King eternal, immortal, invisible,
the only God, be honor and glory for ever and ever. Amen.
*1 Timothy 1:17*

May the God of hope fill you with all joy and peace as you trust in him
so that you may overflow with hope by the power of the Holy Spirit.
*Romans 15:13*

## Sunday

Waiting on Me means directing your attention to Me in hopeful anticipation of what I will do. It entails trusting Me with every fiber of your being, instead of trying to figure things out yourself. Waiting on Me is the way I designed you to live: all day, every day. I created you to stay conscious of Me as you go about your daily duties.

I have promised many blessings to those who wait on Me: *renewed strength,* living above one's circumstances, resurgence of hope, awareness of My continual Presence. Waiting on Me enables you to glorify Me by living in deep dependence on Me, ready to do My will. It also helps you to enjoy Me; *in My Presence is fullness of Joy.*

*Lamentations 3:24–26; Isaiah 40:31;*
*Psalm 16:11 (NKJV)*

## Monday

Stop trying to work things out before their times have come. Accept the limitations of living one day at a time. When something comes to your attention, ask Me whether or not it is part of today's agenda. If it isn't, release it into My care and go on about today's duties. When you follow this practice, there will be a beautiful simplicity about your life: *a time for everything, and everything in its time.*

A life lived close to Me is not complicated or cluttered. When your focus is on My Presence, many things that once troubled you lose their power over you. Though the world around you is messy and confusing, remember that *I have overcome the world. I have told you these things, so that in Me you may have Peace.*

*Ecclesiastes 3:1; John 16:33*

## Tuesday

I am working on your behalf. Bring Me all your concerns, including your dreams. Talk with Me about everything, letting the Light of My Presence shine on your hopes and plans. Spend time allowing My Light to infuse your dreams with life, gradually transforming them into reality. This is a very practical way of collaborating with Me. I, the Creator of the universe, have deigned to co-create with you. Do not try to hurry this process. If you want to work with Me, you have to accept My time frame. Hurry is not in My nature. Abraham and Sarah had to wait many years for the fulfillment of My promise, a son. How their long wait intensified their enjoyment of this child! *Faith is the assurance of things hoped for, perceiving as real fact what is not revealed to the senses.*

*Psalm 36:9; Genesis 21:1–7;*
*Hebrews 11:1 (AMP)*

*Wednesday*

Hope is a golden cord connecting you to heaven. This cord helps you hold your head up high, even when multiple trials are buffeting you. I never leave your side, and I never let go of your hand. But without the cord of hope, your head may slump and your feet may shuffle as you journey uphill with Me. Hope lifts your perspective from your weary feet to the glorious view you can see from the high road. You are reminded that the road we're traveling together is ultimately a highway to heaven. When you consider this radiant destination, the roughness or smoothness of the road ahead becomes much less significant. I am training you to hold in your heart a dual focus: My continual Presence and the hope of heaven.

*Romans 12:12; 1 Thessalonians 5:8;*
*Hebrews 6:18–19*

*Thursday*

Leave outcomes up to Me. Follow Me wherever I lead, without worrying about how it will all turn out. Think of your life as an adventure, with Me as your Guide and Companion. Live in the *now*, concentrating on staying in step with Me. When our path leads to a cliff, be willing to climb it with My help. When we come to a resting place, take time to be refreshed in My Presence. Enjoy the rhythm of life lived close to Me.

You already know the ultimate destination of your journey: your entrance into heaven. So keep your focus on the path just before you, leaving outcomes up to Me.

*Psalm 27:13–14; Exodus 15:13*

# Friday

I am able to do far beyond all that you ask or imagine.
Come to Me with positive expectations, knowing
that there is no limit to what I can accomplish. Ask
My Spirit to control your mind, so that you can think
great thoughts of Me. Do not be discouraged by the fact
that many of your prayers are yet unanswered. Time is
a trainer, teaching you to wait upon Me, to trust Me
in the dark. The more extreme your circumstances, the
more likely you are to see *My Power and Glory* at work
in the situation. Instead of letting difficulties draw you
into worrying, try to view them as setting the scene for
My glorious intervention. Keep your eyes and your
mind wide open to all that I am doing in your life.

*Ephesians 3:20–21; Romans 8:6;*
*Isaiah 40:30–31 (NKJV); Revelation 5:13*

# Saturday

When I give you no special guidance, stay where you are. Concentrate on doing your everyday tasks in awareness of My Presence with you. The Joy of My Presence will shine on you, as you do everything for Me. Thus you invite Me into every aspect of your life. Through collaborating with Me in all things, you allow My Life to merge with yours. This is the secret not only of joyful living but also of victorious living. I designed you to depend on Me moment by moment, recognizing that *apart from Me you can do nothing.*

Be thankful for quiet days, when nothing special seems to be happening. Instead of being bored by the lack of action, use times of routine to seek My Face. Although this is an invisible transaction, it speaks volumes in spiritual realms. Moreover, you are richly blessed when you walk trustingly with Me through the routines of your day.

*Colossians 3:23; John 15:5; Psalm 105:4*

# Week 13

I am ever so near you, hovering over your shoulder, reading every thought. People think that thoughts are fleeting and worthless, but yours are precious to Me.

## Dear Jesus,

This is glorious—yet disconcerting! My thinking is not only the part of me that feels most hidden and secret; it is also the most difficult part of my behavior to master. In relationships with other people I can interact with them while keeping my secret thoughts to myself. Your ability to read my every thought is alarming, but it is also wonderful. It's a relief that there is Someone from whom I cannot hide: Secretiveness breeds loneliness. Moreover, the fact that You care about every aspect of me—even all my thoughts—demonstrates how important I am to You.

Beloved, I know how difficult it is for you to control your thoughts. Your mind is a battleground, and evil spirits work tirelessly to influence your thinking; even deceiving you with intrusive thoughts at times. Your own sinfulness also finds ample expression in your thoughts. You need to stay alert and fight against evil! I fought and died for you, so remember who you are and Whose you are. Thus, you put on the helmet of salvation. This helmet not only protects your mind, it also reminds you of the victory I secured for you on the cross.

Your thoughts are precious to Me because you are My treasure. As soon as your thinking turns My way, I notice and rejoice. The more thoughts you bring to Me, the more you can share in My Joy. I disarm evil thoughts and render them powerless. Then I help you think about things that are true, noble, right, pure, lovely, admirable—excellent and praiseworthy things. Ponder these things, while resting in the Peace of My Presence.

O LORD, you have searched me and you know me. You know when I sit and when I rise; you perceive my thoughts from afar.
*Psalm 139:1–2*

Take the helmet of salvation and the sword of the Spirit, which is the word of God.
*Ephesians 6:17*

Finally, brothers, whatever is true, whatever is noble, whatever is right, whatever is pure, whatever is lovely, whatever is admirable—if anything is excellent or praiseworthy—think about such things.
*Philippians 4:8*

*Sunday*

I want you to be all Mine, filled with the Light of My Presence. I gave everything for you by living as a man, then dying for your sins and living again. Hold back nothing from Me. Bring your most secret thoughts into the Light of My Love. Anything you bring to Me I transform and cleanse from darkness. I know everything about you, far more than you know of yourself. But I restrain My yearning to "fix" you, waiting instead for you to come to Me for help. Imagine the divine restraint this requires, for *I have all Power in heaven and on earth.*

Seek My Face with a teachable spirit. Come into My Presence with thanksgiving, desiring to be transformed.

*Matthew 28:18; Psalm 100:4*

*Monday*

Let My Love seep into the inner recesses of your being. Do not close off any part of yourself from Me. I know you inside and out, so do not try to present a "cleaned-up" self to Me. Wounds that you shut away from the Light of My Love will fester and become wormy. Secret sins that you "hide" from Me can split off and develop lives of their own, controlling you without your realizing it.

Open yourself fully to My transforming Presence. Let My brilliant Love-Light search out and destroy hidden fears. This process requires time alone with Me, as My Love soaks into your innermost being. Enjoy *My perfect Love, which expels every trace of fear.*

**Psalm 139:1–4, 23–24; 1 John 4:18 (AMP)**

# Tuesday

My thoughts are not your thoughts; neither are your ways My ways. As the heavens are higher than the earth, so are My ways and thoughts higher than yours. Remember who I AM when you spend time with Me. Marvel at the wonder of being able to commune with the King of the universe—any time, any place. Never take this amazing privilege for granted!

Though I am vastly higher and greater than you, I am training you to think My thoughts. As you spend time in My Presence, My thoughts gradually form in your mind. My Spirit is the Director of this process. Sometimes He brings Bible verses to mind. Sometimes He enables you to hear Me "speak" directly to you. These communications strengthen you and prepare you for whatever is before you on your life-path. Take time to listen to My voice. Through your sacrifice of precious time, I bless you far more than you dare to ask.

*Isaiah 55:8–9; Colossians 4:2; Psalm 116:17*

## Wednesday

When your sins weigh heavily upon you, come to Me. Confess your wrongdoing, which I know all about before you say a word. Stay in the Light of My Presence, receiving forgiveness, cleansing, and healing. Remember that I have clothed *you in My righteousness*, so nothing can separate you from Me. Whenever you stumble or fall, I am there to help you up.

Man's tendency is to hide from his sin, seeking refuge in the darkness. There he indulges in self-pity, denial, self-righteousness, blaming, and hatred. But *I am the Light of the world*, and My illumination decimates the darkness. Come close to Me and let My Light envelop you, driving out darkness and permeating you with Peace.

*1 John 1:7; Isaiah 61:10; John 8:12*

## Thursday

Let Me control your mind. The mind is the most restless, unruly part of mankind. Long after you have learned the discipline of holding your tongue, your thoughts defy your will and set themselves up against Me. Man is the pinnacle of My creation, and the human mind is wondrously complex. I risked all by granting you freedom to think for yourself. This is a godlike privilege, forever setting you apart from animals and robots. *I made you in My image*, precariously close to deity.

Though My blood has fully redeemed you, your mind is the last bastion of rebellion. Open yourself to My radiant Presence, letting My Light permeate your thinking. *When My Spirit is controlling your mind, you are filled with Life and Peace.*

*Genesis 1:26–27; Romans 8:6*

## Friday

Do not be surprised by the fiery attacks on your mind. When you struggle to find Me and to live in My Peace, don't let discouragement set in. You are engaged in massive warfare, spiritually speaking. The evil one abhors your closeness to Me, and his demonic underlings are determined to destroy our intimacy. When you find yourself in the thick of battle, call upon My Name: "Jesus, help me!" At that instant, the battle becomes Mine; your role is simply to trust Me as I fight for you.

My Name, properly used, has unlimited Power to bless and protect. At the end of time, *every knee will bow (in heaven, on earth, and under the earth), when My Name is proclaimed.* People who have used "Jesus" as a shoddy swear word will fall down in terror on that awesome day. But all those who have drawn near Me through trustingly uttering My Name will be filled with *inexpressible and glorious Joy.* This is your great hope, as you await My return.

*Ephesians 6:12; 1 Samuel 17:47;*
*Philippians 2:9–10; 1 Peter 1:8–9*

*Saturday*

I love you for who you are, not for what you do. Many voices vie for control of your mind, especially when you sit in silence. You must learn to discern what is My voice and what is not. Ask My Spirit to give you this discernment. Many of My children run around in circles, trying to obey the various voices directing their lives. This results in fragmented, frustrating patterns of living. Do not fall into this trap. Walk closely with Me each moment, listening for My directives and enjoying My Companionship. Refuse to let other voices tie you up in knots. *My sheep know My voice and follow Me wherever I lead.*

Ephesians 4:1–6; John 10:4

# Week 14

Bearing your circumstances bravely—even thanking Me for them—is one of the highest forms of praise. This sacrifice of thanksgiving rings golden-toned bells of Joy throughout heavenly realms. On earth, also, your patient suffering sends out ripples of good tidings in ever-widening circles.

## Dear Jesus,

You have been training me in the discipline of thankfulness for a long time. Yet I still find it quite challenging to thank You for suffering—my own or others'. Sometimes, though, I am able to thank You for painful circumstances. This seems unnatural at first, but it is actually quite freeing. When I am able to do this, I find that I relax and feel closer to You. Please help me endure my circumstances bravely—with gratitude.

Beloved, thanking Me for adversity requires a deep level of trust: in My goodness, My mercy, My Love. People who are leaning on their own understanding cannot achieve this depth of trust. So,

handling difficulties courageously involves relinquishing
your demand to understand.

You have experienced personal benefits from
thanking Me for hard situations, but there is more—
much more! Your grateful acceptance of adversity has
major repercussions far beyond yourself: in heaven as
well as on earth. Joy-bells resound in heavenly domains
when suffering believers trust Me enough to give thanks.
Also, your sacrifice of thanksgiving has divine Power
to weaken spiritual strongholds of evil. Moreover,
your patient endurance of suffering can strengthen and
encourage My people on earth.

Sacrifice thank offerings to Me. Tell of My works
with songs of Joy! (Psalm 107:22)

Always giving thanks to God the Father for
everything, in the name of our Lord Jesus Christ.
*Ephesians 5:20*

Trust in the LORD with all your heart
and lean not on your own understanding.
*Proverbs 3:5*

For though we live in the world, we do not wage war as the world
does. The weapons we fight with are not the weapons of the world.
On the contrary, they have divine power to demolish strongholds.
*2 Corinthians 10:3–4*

## Sunday

Let Me teach you thankfulness. Begin by acknowledging that everything—all your possessions and all that you are—belongs to Me. The dawning of each new day is a gift from Me, not to be taken for granted. The earth is vibrantly alive with My blessings, giving vivid testimony to My Presence. If you slow down your pace of life, you can find Me anywhere.

Some of My most precious children have been laid aside in sick beds or shut away in prisons. Others have voluntarily learned the discipline of spending time alone with Me. The secret of being thankful is learning to see everything from My perspective. My world is your classroom. *My Word is a lamp to your feet and a light for your path.*

**Hebrews 12:28–29; Psalm 119:105**

## Monday

Make friends with the problems in your life. Though many things feel random and wrong, remember that I am sovereign over everything. *I can fit everything into a pattern for good,* but only to the extent that you trust Me. Every problem can teach you something, transforming you little by little into the masterpiece I created you to be. The very same problem can become a stumbling block over which you fall, if you react with distrust and defiance. The choice is up to you, and you will have to choose many times each day whether to trust Me or defy Me.

The best way to befriend your problems is to thank Me for them. This simple act opens your mind to the possibility of benefits flowing from your difficulties. You can even give persistent problems nicknames, helping you approach them with familiarity rather than with dread. The next step is to introduce them to Me, so I can embrace them in My loving Presence. Though I may not remove your problems, My wisdom is sufficient to bring good out of every one of them.

*Romans 8:28 (AMP); 1 Corinthians 1:23–24*

## Tuesday

I am calling you to a life of thankfulness. I want all your moments to be punctuated with thanksgiving. The basis for your gratitude is My sovereignty. I am the Creator and Controller of the universe. Heaven and earth are filled with My glorious Presence.

When you criticize or complain, you are acting as if you think *you* could run the world better than I do. From your limited human perspective, it may look as if I'm mismanaging things. But you don't know what I know or see what I see. If I pulled back the curtain to allow you to view heavenly realms, you would understand much more. However, I have designed you to *live by faith, not by sight*. I lovingly shield you from knowing the future or seeing into the spirit world. Acknowledge My sovereignty by *giving thanks in all circumstances*.

*Isaiah 6:3; 2 Corinthians 5:7;*
*1 Thessalonians 5:18*

# Wednesday

Thank Me in the midst of the crucible. When things seem all wrong, look for growth opportunities. Especially, look for areas where you need to let go, leaving your cares in My able hands. Do you trust Me to orchestrate your life events as I choose, or are you still trying to make things go according to *your* will? If you keep trying to carry out your intentions while I am leading you in another direction, you defy your desires.

Be on the lookout for what *I* am doing in your life. Worship Me by living close to Me, *thanking Me in all circumstances.*

*1 Peter 5:6–7; 1 Thessalonians 5:18*

## Thursday

Thank Me for the very things that are troubling you. You are on the brink of rebellion, precariously close to shaking your fist in My Face. You are tempted to indulge in just a little complaining about My treatment of you. But once you step over that line, torrents of rage and self-pity can sweep you away. The best protection against this indulgence is thanksgiving. It is impossible to thank Me and curse Me at the same time.

Thanking Me for trials will feel awkward and contrived at first. But if you persist, your thankful words, prayed in faith, will eventually make a difference in your heart. Thankfulness awakens you to My Presence, which overshadows all your problems.

*Psalm 116:17 (NKJV); Philippians 4:4–6*

## Friday

*Taste and see that I am good.* This command contains an invitation to experience My living Presence. It also contains a promise. The more you experience Me, the more convinced you become of My goodness. This knowledge is essential to your faith-walk. When adversities strike, the human instinct is to doubt My goodness. My ways are mysterious, even to those who know Me intimately. *As the heavens are higher than the earth, so are My ways and thoughts higher than your ways and thoughts.* Do not try to fathom My ways. Instead, spend time enjoying Me and experiencing My goodness.

**Psalm 34:8; Isaiah 55:8–9**

# Saturday

When you worship Me *in spirit and truth*, you join with choirs of angels who are continually before My throne. Though you cannot hear their voices, your praise and thanksgiving are distinctly audible in heaven. Your petitions are also heard, but it is your gratitude that clears the way to My Heart. With the way between us wide open, My blessings fall upon you in rich abundance. The greatest blessing is nearness to Me–abundant Joy and Peace in My Presence. Practice praising and thanking Me continually throughout this day.

*John 4:23–24; Psalm 100:4*

Week 15

> In union with Me you are complete. In closeness to Me, you are transformed more and more into the one I designed you to be.

## Dear Jesus,

I often feel incomplete, as if some vital part of me is missing. When this is just a feeling—not a conscious thought—I respond in many unproductive ways: foraging for food, looking for entertainment, searching for myself in the mirror, and so on. All the while, You are with me, patiently waiting for me to remember You. If I continue to go my own way—seeking satisfaction where there is none—I become increasingly frustrated. My agitated condition makes it hard for me to turn back to You, the only One who can complete me. I have found, though, that it is never too late to cry out, "Help me, Jesus!"

Beloved, when a child of Mine calls out to Me, I never fail to respond. I may not provide instant relief, as if I were just a genie, but I go to work immediately, setting in motion the conditions you need. I help you gain awareness of what you have been doing: seeking fulfillment in worldly ways. In response to your neediness, I offer you My glorious riches. When you have settled down enough to see clearly, I proffer Myself to you. I invite you to come near Me, where you can find completeness.

As you center your attention on Me, I draw closer to you. While you rest in the rarified air of My Presence, I bless you with My Peace. Though you are just a jar of clay, I fill you with My treasure: the Light of the knowledge of My Glory. This divine Light fills you to the brim—making you complete. It also transforms you, bit by bit, into the masterpiece I designed you to be.

Perseverance must finish its work so that you may
be mature and complete, not lacking anything.
*James 1:4*

He fulfills the desires of those who fear him;
he hears their cry and saves them.
*Psalm 145:19*

Submit yourselves, then, to God. Resist the devil, and he will flee
from you. Come near to God and he will come near to you.
*James 4:7–8*

For God, who said, "Let light shine out of darkness," made his light
shine in our hearts to give us the light of the knowledge of the glory
of God in the face of Christ. But we have this treasure in jars of clay to
show that this all-surpassing power is from God and not from us.
*2 Corinthians 4:6–7*

*Sunday*

Rest in My radiant Presence. The world around you seems to spin faster and faster, till everything is a blur. Yet there is a cushion of calm at the center of your life, where you live in union with Me. Return to this soothing Center as often as you can, for this is where you are energized: filled with My Love, Joy, and Peace.

The world is a needy place; do not go there for sustenance. Instead, come to Me. Learn to depend on Me alone, and your weakness will become saturated with My Power. When you find your completeness in Me, you can help other people without using them to meet your own needs. Live in the Light of My Presence, and your light will shine brightly into the lives of others.

*Galatians 5:22; 1 John 4:12*

Monday

Your *needs and My riches* are a perfect fit. I never meant for you to be self-sufficient. Instead, I designed you to need Me not only for daily bread but also for fulfillment of deep yearnings. I carefully crafted your longings and feelings of incompleteness, to point you to Me. Therefore, do not try to bury or deny these feelings. Beware also of trying to pacify these longings with lesser gods: people, possessions, power.

Come to Me in all your neediness, with defenses down and with desire to be blessed. As you spend time in My Presence, your deepest longings are fulfilled. Rejoice in your neediness, which enables you to find intimate completion in Me.

*Philippians 4:19; Colossians 2:2–3*

## Tuesday

In Me you have everything. In Me you are complete. Your capacity to experience Me is increasing, through My removal of debris and clutter from your heart. As your yearning for Me increases, other desires are gradually lessening. Since I am infinite and abundantly accessible to you, desiring Me above all else is the best way to live.

It is impossible for you to have a need that I cannot meet. After all, I created you and everything that is. The world is still at My beck and call, though it often appears otherwise. Do not be fooled by appearances. *Things that are visible are brief and fleeting, while things that are invisible are everlasting.*

**Ephesians 3:20;**
**2 Corinthians 4:18 (AMP)**

# Wednesday

When some basic need is lacking—time, energy, money—consider yourself blessed. Your very lack is an opportunity to latch onto Me in unashamed dependence. When you begin a day with inadequate resources, you must concentrate your efforts on the present moment. This is where you are meant to live—in the present; it is the place where I always await you. Awareness of your inadequacy is a rich blessing, training you to rely wholeheartedly on Me.

The truth is that self-sufficiency is a myth perpetuated by pride and temporary success. Health and wealth can disappear instantly, as can life itself. Rejoice in your insufficiency, knowing that *My Power is made perfect in weakness*.

*James 1:2; 2 Corinthians 12:9 (NASB)*

## Thursday

Seek My Face, and you will find fulfillment of your deepest longings. My world is filled with beautiful things; they are meant to be pointers to Me, reminders of My abiding Presence. The earth still declares My Glory to those who have eyes that see and ears that hear.

You had a darkened mind before you sought Me wholeheartedly. I chose to pour My Light into you, so that you can be a beacon to others. There is no room for pride in this position. Your part is to reflect *My* Glory. I am the Lord!

*Psalm 105:4; Psalm 19:1–2; Isaiah 60:2*

## Friday

Come to Me continually. I am meant to be the Center of your consciousness, the *Anchor of your soul*. Your mind will wander from Me, but the question is how far you allow it to wander. An anchor on a short rope lets a boat drift only slightly before the taut line tugs the boat back toward the center. Similarly, as you drift away from Me, My Spirit within you gives a tug, prompting you to return to Me. As you become increasingly attuned to My Presence, the length of rope on your soul's Anchor is shortened. You wander only a short distance before feeling that inner tug—telling you to return to your true Center in Me.

*Hebrews 6:19; 1 John 2:28; Matthew 22:37*

*Saturday*

I designed you to live in union with Me. This union does not negate who you are; it actually makes you more fully yourself. When you try to live independently of Me, you experience emptiness and dissatisfaction. You may *gain the whole world* and yet lose everything that really counts.

Find fulfillment through living close to Me, yielding to My purposes for you. Though I may lead you along paths that feel alien to you, trust that I know what I am doing. If you follow Me wholeheartedly, you will discover facets of yourself that were previously hidden. I know you intimately—far better than you know yourself. In union with Me, you are complete. In closeness to Me, you are transformed more and more into the one I designed you to be.

*Mark 8:36; Psalm 139:13–16;*
*2 Corinthians 3:17–18*

# Week 16

> Instead of dreading difficulties that may or may not occur, view this day as a sacred adventure to be shared with Me.

## Dear Jesus,

My heart delights in Your invitation to live this day as a sacred adventure. You are my King of kings, and I long to live in a manner that displays my adoption into Your royal family. You are also my Lord of lords, so anything shared with You is sacred. I admit, though, that my mind is often preoccupied with ordinary matters and concerns. When a new day stands open before me, I scan it for difficulties that may occur, wondering if I'll be able to cope. This is the natural bent of my mind: an earth-bound focus.

Beloved, it is natural for your mind to be drawn toward mundane matters. But you are capable of so much more than that! I created you in own My image, with incredible abilities given only to mankind. When you became a believer, I infused My Spirit into your innermost being. The combination of

My image and My Spirit in you is powerful—making you fit for greatness.

I want you to begin each day viewing yourself as a chosen warrior, ready to go into battle. Of course, there will be difficulties, but they need not be your focus. Put on the full armor I have provided, and you will be ready for whatever battles you have to fight. When you are engaged in combat, keep looking to Me for strength and guidance. Remember that you and I together can handle whatever difficulties come your way. Abandon yourself to the challenges I have chosen for you. Then you will find your days increasingly devoted to sacred adventures shared with Me—your King!

God, the blessed and only Ruler, the King of kings and Lord of lords, who alone is immortal and who lives in unapproachable light, whom no one has seen or can see. To him be honor and might forever. Amen.
*1 Timothy 6:15–16*

And if the Spirit of him who raised Jesus from the dead is living in you, he who raised Christ from the dead will also give life to your mortal bodies through his Spirit, who lives in you.
*Romans 8:11*

Therefore put on the full armor of God, so that when the day of evil comes, you may be able to stand your ground, and after you have done everything, to stand.
*Ephesians 6:13*

*Sunday*

Refuse to worry! In this world there will always be something enticing you to worry. That is the nature of a fallen, fractured planet: Things are not as they should be. So the temptation to be anxious is constantly with you, trying to worm its way into your mind. The best defense is *continual communication with Me, richly seasoned with thanksgiving.* Awareness of My Presence fills your mind with Light and Peace, leaving no room for fear. This awareness lifts you up above your circumstances, enabling you to see problems from My perspective. Live close to Me! Together we can keep the wolves of worry at bay.

*Luke 12:25–26; 1 Thessalonians 5:16–18*

## Monday

As you look into the day that stretches out before you, you see many choice-points along the way. The myriad possibilities these choices present can confuse you. Draw your mind back to the threshold of this day, where I stand beside you, lovingly preparing you for what is ahead.

You must make your choices one at a time, since each is contingent upon the decision that precedes it. Instead of trying to create a mental map of your path through this day, focus on My loving Presence with you. I will equip you as you go, so that you can handle whatever comes your way. Trust Me to supply what you need when you need it.

*Lamentations 3:22–26; Psalm 34:8 (NKJV)*

## Tuesday

If you learn to trust Me—really trust Me—with your whole being, then nothing can separate you from My Peace. Everything you endure can be put to good use by allowing it to train you in trusting Me. This is how you foil the works of evil, growing in grace through the very adversity that was meant to harm you. Joseph was a prime example of this divine reversal, declaring to his brothers: *"You meant evil against me, but God meant it for good."*

Do not fear what this day, or any day, may bring your way. Concentrate on trusting Me and on doing what needs to be done. Relax in My sovereignty, remembering that I go before you, as well as with you, into each day. *Fear no evil,* for I can bring good out of every situation you will ever encounter.

*Genesis 50:20 (NASB); Psalm 23:4*

## Wednesday

Do not let any set of circumstances intimidate you. The more challenging your day, the more of My Power I place at your disposal. You seem to think that I empower you equally each day, but this is not so. Your tendency upon awakening is to assess the difficulties ahead of you, measuring them against your average strength. This is an exercise in unreality.

I know what each of your days will contain, and I empower you accordingly. The degree to which I strengthen you on a given day is based mainly on two variables: the difficulty of your circumstances, and your willingness to depend on Me for help. Try to view challenging days as opportunities to receive more of My Power than usual. Look to Me for all that you need, and watch to see what I will do. *As your day, so shall your strength be.*

*Ephesians 1:18–20; Psalm 105:4;*
*Deuteronomy 33:25 (NKJV)*

*Thursday*

I am involved in each moment of your life. I have carefully mapped out every inch of your journey through this day, even though much of it may feel haphazard. Because the world is in a fallen condition, things always seem to be unraveling around the edges. Expect to find trouble in this day. At the same time, trust that *My way is perfect,* even in the midst of such messy imperfection.

Stay conscious of Me as you go through this day, remembering that I never leave your side. Let the Holy Spirit guide you step by step, protecting you from unnecessary trials and equipping you to get through whatever must be endured. As you trudge through the sludge of this fallen world, keep your mind in heavenly places with Me. Thus the Light of My Presence shines on you, giving you Peace and Joy that circumstances cannot touch.

**Psalm 18:30; Isaiah 41:13**

*Friday*

Welcome challenging times as opportunities to trust Me. You have Me beside you and My Spirit within you, so no set of circumstances is too much for you to handle. When the path before you is dotted with difficulties, beware of measuring your strength against those challenges. That calculation is certain to riddle you with anxiety. Without Me, you wouldn't make it past the first hurdle!

The way to walk through demanding days is to grip My hand tightly and stay in close communication with Me. Let your thoughts and spoken words be richly flavored with trust and thankfulness. Regardless of the day's problems, *I can keep you in perfect Peace* as you stay close to Me.

*James 1:2; Philippians 4:13; Isaiah 26:3*

## Saturday

As you get out of bed in the morning, be aware of My Presence with you. You may not be thinking clearly yet, but I am. Your early morning thoughts tend to be anxious ones until you get connected with Me. Invite Me into your thoughts by whispering My Name. Suddenly your day brightens and feels more user-friendly. You cannot dread a day that is vibrant with My Presence.

You gain confidence through knowing that I am with you—that you face nothing alone. Anxiety stems from asking the wrong question: "If such and such happens, can I handle it?" The true question is not whether you can cope with whatever happens, but whether you and I together can handle anything that occurs. It is this you-and-I-together factor that gives you confidence to face the day cheerfully.

*Psalm 5:3; Psalm 63:1 (NKJV); Philippians 4:13*

# Week 17

> My Light shines most brightly through
> believers who trust Me in the dark.
> That kind of trust is supernatural:
> a production of My indwelling Spirit.

## Dear Jesus,

I love walking in the Light with You. I am a creature who craves light—sunlight and even artificial light, but especially the Light of Your holy Presence. I trust You easily when there's plenty of light in my world. Trusting You in the dark is another matter altogether; there's a kind of desperation to it—clinging to You as if my life depended on it.

## Beloved,

growing in grace is all about trusting Me: in good times, in bad times, at all times. I am Lord over all your circumstances, so I want to be involved in every aspect of your life. One of the best ways of connecting with Me—here and now—is trusting Me in the very situation where you find yourself. When your world seems dark and you trust Me anyway, My Light shines brightly through you. You may not be aware of this illumination, but it is visible to many: both in heavenly realms and on earth. Your display of transcendent trust weakens spiritual forces of evil. People around you are strengthened and blessed by My supernatural Light showing through you.

Clinging to Me in the dark feels like an act requiring all your willpower. Exerting your will is definitely important, but there is more: My hand has an eternal grip on yours. I will never let go of you! Moreover, My indwelling Spirit empowers you to keep hanging on. When you feel on the brink of giving up, cry out for His assistance: "Help me, Holy Spirit!" This brief prayer enables you to tap into His vast Power. Be encouraged by knowing that though you may see only darkness, My Light is shining through you in surpassing splendor!

> But if we walk in the light, as he is in the light,
> we have fellowship with one another, and the
> blood of Jesus, his Son, purifies us from all sin.
> **1 John 1:7**

> Trust in him at all times, O people;
> pour out your hearts to him, for God is our refuge.
> **Psalm 62:8**

> Even there Your hand shall lead me,
> and Your right hand shall hold me.
> **Psalm 139:10 NKJV**

## Sunday

Seek Me with your whole being. I desire to be found by you, and I orchestrate the events of your life with that purpose in mind. When things go well and you are blessed, you can feel Me smiling on you. When you encounter rough patches along your life-journey, trust that My Light is still shining upon you. My reasons for allowing these adversities may be shrouded in mystery, but My continual Presence with you is an absolute promise. Seek Me in good times; seek Me in hard times. You will find Me watching over you all the time.

*Deuteronomy 4:29; Hebrews 10:23;*
*Psalm 145:20*

# Monday

I *am the Light of the world.* Men crawl through their lives cursing the darkness, but all the while I am shining brightly. I desire each of My followers to be a Light-bearer. The Holy Spirit who lives in you can shine from your face, making Me visible to people around you. Ask My Spirit to live through you, as you wend your way through this day. Hold My hand in joyful trust, for I never leave your side. The Light of My Presence is shining upon you. Brighten up the world by reflecting who I am.

*John 8:12; Matthew 5:14–16;*
*2 Corinthians 3:18; Exodus 3:14*

*Tuesday*

Hold My hand—and trust. So long as you are conscious of My Presence with you, all is well. It is virtually impossible to stumble while walking in the Light with Me. I designed you to enjoy Me above all else. You find the deepest fulfillment of your heart in Me alone.

Fearful, anxious thoughts melt away in the Light of My Presence. When you turn away from Me, you are vulnerable to the darkness that is always at work in the world. Don't be surprised by how easily you sin when you forget to cling to My hand. In the world, dependency is seen as immaturity. But in My kingdom, dependence on Me is a prime measure of maturity.

**Isaiah 41:10; Psalm 62:5–6**

# Wednesday

In closeness to Me, you are safe. In the intimacy of My Presence, you are energized. No matter where you are in the world, you know you belong when you sense My nearness. Ever since the Fall, man has experienced a gaping emptiness that only My Presence can fill. I designed you for close communication with your Creator. How I enjoyed walking in the garden with Adam and Eve, before the evil one deceived them!

When you commune with Me in the garden of your heart, both you and I are blessed. This is My way of living in the world—through you! Together we will push back the darkness, for *I am the Light of the world.*

**Psalm 32:7; Genesis 3:8–9; John 8:12**

## Thursday

Seek to live in My Love, which *covers a multitude of sins:* both yours and others'. Wear My Love like a cloak of Light, covering you from head to toe. Have no fear, for *perfect Love decimates fear.* Look at other people through lenses of Love; see them from My perspective. This is how you walk in the Light, and it pleases Me.

I want My Body of believers to be radiant with the Light of My Presence. How I grieve when pockets of darkness increasingly dim the Love-Light. Return to Me, your *First Love!* Gaze at Me in the splendor of holiness, and My Love will once again envelop you in Light.

*1 Peter 4:8; 1 John 4:18; Revelation 2:4*

## Friday

Let My Presence override everything you experience. Like a luminous veil of Light, I hover over you and everything around you. I am training you to stay conscious of Me in each situation you encounter.

When the patriarch Jacob ran away from his enraged brother, he went to sleep on a stone pillow in a land that seemed desolate. But after dreaming about heaven and angels and promises of My Presence, he awoke and exclaimed· "Surely the Lord is in this place, and I was not aware of it." His discovery was not only for him but for all who seek Me. Whenever you feel distant from Me, say: "Surely the Lord is in this place!" Then, ask Me to give you awareness of My Presence. This is a prayer that I delight to answer.

*Psalm 31:20; Genesis 28:11–16*

*Saturday*

Taste and see that I am good. The more intimately you experience Me, the more convinced you become of My goodness. I am *the Living One who sees you* and longs to participate in your life. I am training you to find Me in each moment and to be a channel of My loving Presence. Sometimes My blessings come to you in mysterious ways: through pain and trouble. At such times you can know My goodness only through your trust in Me. Understanding will fail you, but trust will keep you close to Me.

Thank Me for the gift of My Peace, a gift of such immense proportions that you cannot fathom its depth or breadth. When I appeared to My disciples after the resurrection, it was Peace that I communicated first of all. I knew this was their deepest need: to calm their fears and clear their minds. I also speak Peace to you, for I know your anxious thoughts. Listen to Me! Tune out other voices, so that you can hear Me more clearly. I designed you to dwell in Peace all day, every day. Draw near to Me; receive My Peace.

*Psalm 34:8; Genesis 16:13–14 (AMP); John 20:19*

# Week 18

Remember that you live in a fallen world: an abnormal world tainted by sin. Much frustration and failure result from your seeking perfection in this life.

*Dear Jesus,*

I know I live in a fallen world, but sometimes I slip into denial of that truth. I'm still driven to seek perfection where it can never be found—this world. I waste so much time and energy trying to do things perfectly, when simply getting them done would be sufficient. This leads not only to frustration but also, at times, to its close ally: anger. Please help me break out of this self-defeating behavior.

*Beloved,* your yearning for perfection is not bad in itself. I placed this longing in your heart so you would search for Me. However, your heart also contains many effects of the Fall. As a result, you often seek perfection apart from Me. This sets you on a path of frustration and failure—sometimes even idolatry. You can always *return* to Me by choosing to seek Me first and foremost. As you do so, I set your feet on a rock and give you a firm place to stand. I also put a new song in your mouth: a hymn of praise.

Do not try to stifle your longing for perfection. It serves a paramount purpose—pointing you not only to Me but also to your future, eternal home. Your unsatisfied yearnings can awaken you to the radiant perfection awaiting you in heaven. So, let the frustration of living in a fallen world remind you that you originated in a perfect place (Eden) and you're on the way to an inexpressibly glorious place—heaven!

He lifted me out of the slimy pit, out of the mud and mire;
he set my feet on a rock and gave me a firm place to stand.
He put a new song in my mouth, a hymn of praise to our God.
Many will see and fear and put their trust in the LORD.
*Psalm 40:2–3*

Now the LORD God had planted a garden in the east, in Eden;
and there he put the man he had formed.
*Genesis 2:8*

But our citizenship is in heaven. And we eagerly await a Savior
from there, the Lord Jesus Christ, who, by the power that enables
him to bring everything under his control, will transform our
lowly bodies so that they will be like his glorious body.
*Philippians 3:20–21*

*Sunday*

Bring Me your mind for rest and renewal. Let Me infuse My Presence into your thoughts. As your mind stops racing, your body relaxes and you regain awareness of Me. This awareness is vital to your spiritual well-being; it is your lifeline, spiritually speaking.

There are actually more than four dimensions in this world where you live. In addition to the three dimensions of space and the one of time, there is the dimension of openness to My Presence. This dimension transcends the others, giving you glimpses of heaven while you still reside on earth. This was part of My original design for mankind. Adam and Eve used to walk with Me in the garden, before their expulsion from Eden. I want you to walk with Me in the garden of your heart, where I have taken up permanent residence.

*Genesis 3:8; Psalm 89:15*

## Monday

I am calling you to a life of constant communion with Me. Basic training includes learning to live above your circumstances, even while interacting on that cluttered plane of life. You yearn for a simplified lifestyle, so that your communication with Me can be uninterrupted. But I challenge you to relinquish the fantasy of an uncluttered world. Accept each day just as it comes, and find Me in the midst of it all.

Talk with Me about every aspect of your day, including your feelings. Remember that your ultimate goal is not to control or fix everything around you; it is to keep communing with Me. A successful day is one in which you have stayed in touch with Me, even if many things remain undone at the end of the day. Do not let your to-do list (written or mental) become an idol directing your life. Instead, ask My Spirit to guide you moment by moment. He will keep you close to Me.

*1 Thessalonians 5:17; Proverbs 3:6*

## Tuesday

Do not long for the absence of problems in your life. That is an unrealistic goal, since *in this world you will have trouble.* You have an eternity of problem-free living reserved for you in heaven. Rejoice in that inheritance, which no one can take away from you, but do not seek your heaven on earth.

Begin each day anticipating problems, asking Me to equip you for whatever difficulties you will encounter. The best equipping is My living Presence, *My hand that never lets go of yours.* Discuss everything with Me. Take a lighthearted view of trouble, seeing it as a challenge that you and I together can handle. Remember that I am on your side, and *I have overcome the world.*

*John 16:33; Isaiah 41:13; Philippians 4:13*

# Wednesday

I am the firm foundation on which you can dance and sing and celebrate My Presence. This is My high and holy calling for you; receive it as a precious gift. *Glorifying and enjoying Me* is a higher priority than maintaining a tidy, structured life. Give up your striving to keep everything under control—an impossible task and a waste of precious energy.

My guidance for each of My children is unique. That's why listening to Me is so vital for your well-being. Let Me prepare you for the day that awaits you and point you in the right direction. I am with you continually, so don't be intimidated by fear. Though it stalks you, it cannot harm you, as long as you cling to My hand. Keep your eyes on Me, enjoying Peace in My Presence.

*Psalm 5:11; Ephesians 3:20–21;*
*Jude 24–25; Joshua 1:5*

*Thursday*

Learn to laugh at yourself more freely. Don't take yourself or your circumstances so seriously. Relax and know that I am *God with you*. When you desire My will above all else, life becomes much less threatening. Stop trying to monitor My responsibilities—things that are beyond your control. Find freedom by accepting the boundaries of your domain.

Laughter lightens your load and lifts your heart into heavenly places. Your laughter rises to heaven and blends with angelic melodies of praise. Just as parents delight in the laughter of their children, so I delight in hearing My children laugh. I rejoice when you trust Me enough to enjoy your life lightheartedly.

Do not miss the Joy of My Presence by carrying the weight of the world on your shoulders. Rather, *take My yoke upon you and learn from Me. My yoke is comfortable and pleasant; My burden is light and easily borne.*

*Proverbs 17:22; Proverbs 31:25;*
*Matthew 1:23; Matthew 11:28–30 (AMP)*

## Friday

Remember that you live in a fallen world: an abnormal world tainted by sin. Much frustration and failure result from your seeking perfection in this life. There is nothing perfect in this world except Me. That is why closeness to Me satisfies deep yearnings and fills you with Joy.

I have planted longing for perfection in every human heart. This is a good desire, which I alone can fulfill. But most people seek this fulfillment in other people and earthly pleasures or achievements. Thus they create idols, before which they bow down. *I will have no other gods before Me!* Make Me the deepest desire of your heart. Let Me fulfill your yearning for perfection.

**Exodus 20:3; Psalm 37:4**

*Saturday*

Give up the illusion that you deserve a problem-free life. Part of you is still hungering for the resolution of all difficulties. This is a false hope! As I told My disciples, *in the world you will have trouble*. Link your hope not to problem solving in this life but to the promise of an eternity of problem-free life in heaven. Instead of seeking perfection in this fallen world, pour your energy into seeking Me: the Perfect One.

It is possible to enjoy Me and glorify Me in the midst of adverse circumstances. In fact, My Light shines most brightly through believers who trust Me in the dark. That kind of trust is supernatural: a production of My indwelling Spirit. When things seem all wrong, trust Me anyway. I am much less interested in right circumstances than in right responses to whatever comes your way.

*John 16:33; Psalm 112:4, 7*

# Week 19

As you spend time in My Presence,
My thoughts gradually form in your mind.
My Spirit is the Director of this process.

## Dear Jesus,

There are so many influences on my mind! I'm
thankful for Your Spirit, who infuses Life and Peace into
my mind. If I didn't have the Spirit's help, my thoughts
would be savagely roaming the landscape of my brain—
searching for satisfaction. Even so, my thinking is often
unruly. I long to think Your thoughts more and more.

Beloved, I know even better than you the contents
of your thoughts. Your mind is a spiritual
battlefield. That's why I urge you to stay alert! When
you spend time listening to Me, you need to begin with
prayer for protection. The evil one is *the father of lies*;
his deceptions can worm their way into your mind if
you let down your guard. When you ask for protection,
always pray in My Name, because I defeated the devil
utterly on the cross!

I'm pleased that you desire to think My thoughts. Having prayed for protection, you should also ask the Holy Spirit to help you listen well. He is the Director of this listening adventure. Remain alert while you listen, ready to reject anything inconsistent with biblical truth. As My thoughts gradually form in your mind, you may find it helpful to write them down. Thank Me for what you have received, and continue to seek the help of My Spirit. Don't become overly focused on writing. The process—listening to Me under the direction of My Spirit—is more precious than the product: what you write. As you spend time focusing on Me, you will grow not only closer to Me but also more like Me.

The mind of sinful man is death,
but the mind controlled by the Spirit is life and peace.
*Romans 8:6*

Be self-controlled and alert. Your enemy the devil prowls
around like a roaring lion looking for someone to devour.
*1 Peter 5:8*

He [the devil] was a murderer from the beginning, not holding
to the truth, for there is no truth in him. When he lies, he speaks
his native language, for he is a liar and the father of lies.

*John 8:44*

*Sunday*

I am Life and Light in abundance. As you spend time "soaking" in My Presence, you are energized and lightened. Through communing with Me, you transfer your heavy burdens to My strong shoulders. By gazing at Me, you gain My perspective on your life. This time alone with Me is essential for unscrambling your thoughts and smoothing out the day before you.

Be willing to fight for this precious time with Me. Opposition comes in many forms: your own desire to linger in bed; the evil one's determination to distract you from Me; the pressure of family, friends, and your own inner critic to spend your time more productively. As you grow in your desire to please Me above all else, you gain strength to resist these opponents. *Delight yourself in Me, for I am the deepest Desire of your heart.*

**Psalm 48:9; Deuteronomy 33:12; Psalm 37:4**

*Monday*

Spending time alone with Me is essential for your well-being. It is not a luxury or an option; it is a necessity. Therefore, do not feel guilty about taking time to be with Me. Remember that Satan is *the accuser of believers.* He delights in heaping guilt feelings upon you, especially when you are enjoying My Presence. When you feel Satan's arrows of accusation, you are probably on the right track. Use your *shield of faith* to protect yourself from him. Talk with Me about what you are experiencing, and ask Me to show you the way forward. *Resist the devil, and he will flee from you. Come near to Me, and I will come near to you.*

*Revelation 12:10; Ephesians 6:16;*
*James 4:7–8*

## Tuesday

The Peace that I give you transcends your intellect. When most of your mental energy goes into efforts to figure things out, you are unable to receive this glorious gift. I look into your mind and see thoughts spinning round and round: going nowhere, accomplishing nothing. All the while, My Peace hovers over you, searching for a place to land.

Be still in My Presence, inviting Me to control your thoughts. Let My Light soak into your mind and heart, until you are aglow with My very Being. This is the most effective way to receive My Peace.

*2 Thessalonians 3:16; Job 22:21*

## Wednesday

Trust Me and don't be afraid, for I am your Strength
and Song. Do not let fear dissipate your energy.
Instead, invest your energy in trusting Me and singing
My Song. The battle for control of your mind is fierce,
and years of worry have made you vulnerable to the
enemy. Therefore, you need to be vigilant in guarding
your thoughts. Do not despise this weakness in
yourself, since I am using it to draw you closer to Me.
Your constant need for Me creates an intimacy that
is well worth all the effort. You are not alone in this
struggle for your mind. My Spirit living within you is
ever ready to help in this striving. *Ask Him to control
your mind; He will bless you with Life and Peace.*

**Isaiah 12:2; Romans 8:6**

## Thursday

Trust Me in all your thoughts. I know that some thoughts are unconscious or semiconscious, and I do not hold you responsible for those. But you can direct conscious thoughts much more than you may realize. Practice thinking in certain ways—trusting Me, thanking Me—and those thoughts become more natural. Reject negative or sinful thoughts as soon as you become aware of them. Don't try to hide them from Me; confess them and leave them with Me. Go on your way lightheartedly. This method of controlling your thoughts will keep your mind in My Presence and your feet on the *path of Peace*.

*Psalm 20:7; 1 John 1:9; Luke 1:79*

# Friday

Let the dew of My Presence refresh your mind and heart. So many, many things vie for your attention in this complex world of instant communication. The world has changed enormously since I first gave the command to *be still and know that I am God*. However, this timeless truth is essential for the well-being of your soul. As dew refreshes grass and flowers during the stillness of the night, so My Presence revitalizes you as you sit quietly with Me.

A refreshed, revitalized mind is able to sort out what is important and what is not. In its natural condition, your mind easily gets stuck on trivial matters. Like the spinning wheels of a car trapped in mud, the cogs of your brain spin impotently when you focus on a trivial thing. As soon as you start communicating with Me about the matter, your thoughts gain traction and you can move on to more important things. Communicate with Me continually, and I will put My thoughts into your mind.

*Psalm 46:10; Luke 10:39–42;*
*1 Corinthians 14:33 (NKJV)*

## Saturday

I am the Truth: the One who came to *set you free.*
As the Holy Spirit controls your mind and actions
more fully, you become free in Me. You are increasingly
released to become the one I created you to be. This is a
work that I do in you as you yield to My Spirit. I can do
My best handiwork when you sit in the stillness of My
Presence, focusing your entire being on Me.

Let My thoughts burst freely upon your
consciousness, stimulating abundant Life. *I am the Way
and the Truth and the Life.* As you follow Me, I lead you
along paths of newness: ways you have never imagined.
Don't worry about what is on the road up ahead. I want
you to find your security in knowing Me, the One who
died to *set you free.*

John 8:32; Philippians 2:13; John 14:6

# Week 20

> Walk with Me in holy trust, responding
> to My initiatives rather than trying to
> make things fit your plans.

Dear Jesus,

Thank You for making crystal-clear the choice I face many times each day: responding to Your initiatives in my life versus trying to force things into my plans. When I choose responsiveness, I gain closeness to You and ready access to Your resources. When I try to make things fit into my plans, I usually become frustrated and anxious. In spite of these negative consequences, however, I continue to feel a magnetic pull toward the planning path. This sabotages my deep desire to walk in Your ways, responding wholeheartedly to what You have prepared.

Beloved, I am blessed by your longing to walk in My ways, even when your behavior doesn't line up with that desire. This is really an issue of trust. There is nothing wrong with making plans, but you must not trust in them more than in Me.

I am calling you to walk with Me in holy trust. "Holy" means "set apart for sacred use." Your primary purpose in this life is to be available for sacred use: ready to do My will. When you get so focused on your plans that you hardly see anything else, you are unavailable to Me. If you start feeling frustrated or distant from Me, take time to seek My Face. Open yourself to My loving Presence. The magnetic attraction of My Love will empower you to resist the pull of your planning path. This frees you to respond to My initiatives: joining in the things I have already set in motion. For you are My own handiwork, born anew to do those good works I planned beforehand for you—taking paths I prepared ahead of time. Thus you live the good life that I prearranged and made ready for you

In his heart a man plans his course,
but the LORD determines his steps.
*Proverbs 16:9*

The LORD is good, a refuge in times of trouble.
He cares for those who trust in him.
*Nahum 1:7*

For we are God's [own] handiwork (His workmanship), recreated in
Christ Jesus, [born anew] that we may do those good works which
God predestined (planned beforehand) for us [taking paths which
He prepared ahead of time], that we should walk in them [living the
good life which He prearranged and made ready for us to live].
*Ephesians 2:10 AMP*

# Sunday

I *am the Potter; you are My clay.* I designed you before the foundation of the world. I arrange the events of each day to form you into this preconceived pattern. My everlasting Love is at work in every event of your life. On some days your will and Mine flow smoothly together. You tend to feel in control of your life when our wills are in harmony. On other days you feel as if you are swimming upstream, against the current of My purposes. When that happens, stop and seek My Face. The opposition you feel may be from Me, or it may be from the evil one.

Talk with Me about what you are experiencing. Let My Spirit guide you through treacherous waters. As you move through the turbulent stream with Me, let circumstances mold you into the one I desire you to be. Say *yes* to your Potter as you go through this day.

*Isaiah 64:8; Psalm 27:8*

## Monday

Come to Me with your plans held in abeyance. *Worship Me in spirit and in truth*, allowing My Glory to permeate your entire being. Trust Me enough to let Me guide you through this day, accomplishing My purposes in My timing. Subordinate your myriad plans to My Master Plan. I am sovereign over every aspect of your life!

The challenge continually before you is to trust Me and search for My way through each day. Do not blindly follow your habitual route, or you will miss what I have prepared for you. *As the heavens are higher than the earth, so are My ways higher than your ways and My thoughts than your thoughts.*

**John 4:24; Isaiah 55:8–9 (NKJV)**

*Tuesday*

Rest in Me, My child. Give your mind a break from planning and trying to anticipate what will happen. *Pray continually,* asking My Spirit to take charge of the details of this day. Remember that you are on a journey with Me. When you try to peer into the future and plan for every possibility, you ignore your constant Companion who sustains you moment by moment. As you gaze anxiously into the distance, you don't even feel the strong grip of My hand holding yours. How foolish you are, My child!

Remembrance of Me is a daily discipline. Never lose sight of My Presence with you. This will keep you resting in Me all day, every day.

*1 Thessalonians 5:17; Psalm 62:5*

## Wednesday

Relax and let Me lead you through this day. I have everything under control: My control. You tend to peer anxiously into the day that is before you, trying to figure out what to do, and when. Meanwhile, the phone or the doorbell rings, and you have to reshuffle your plans. All that planning ties you up in knots and distracts you from Me. Attentiveness to Me is not only for your quiet time, but for all your time. As you look to Me, I show you what to do now and next.

Vast quantities of time and energy are wasted in obsessive planning. When you let *Me* direct your steps, you are set free to enjoy Me and to find what I have prepared for you this day.

*Psalm 32:8; Psalm 119:35; Psalm 143:8*

*Thursday*

Stay calmly conscious of Me today, no matter what. Remember that I go before you as well as with you into the day. Nothing takes Me by surprise. I will not allow circumstances to overwhelm you, so long as you look to Me. I will help you cope with whatever the moment presents. Collaborating with Me brings *blessings that far outweigh all your troubles.* Awareness of My Presence contains Joy that can endure all eventualities.

*Psalm 23:1–4 (NKJV); 2 Corinthians 4:16–17*

# Friday

Rest in the stillness of My Presence while I prepare you for this day. Let the radiance of My Glory shine upon you, as you wait on Me in confident trust. *Be still and know that I am God.* There is both a passive and an active side to trusting Me. As you rest in My Presence, focusing on Me, I quietly build bonds of trust between us. When you respond to the circumstances of your life with affirmations of trust, you actively participate in this process.

I am always with you, so you have no reason to be afraid. Your fear often manifests itself in excessive planning. Your mind is so accustomed to this pattern of thinking that you are only now becoming aware of how pervasive it is and how much it hinders your intimacy with Me. Repent of this tendency and resist it, whenever you realize you are wandering down this well-worn path. Return to My Presence, which always awaits you in the present moment. I accept you back with *no condemnation.*

**Psalm 46:10; Romans 8:1**

## Saturday

Hold My hand, and walk joyously with Me through this day. Together we will savor the pleasures and endure the difficulties it brings. Be on the lookout for everything I have prepared for you: stunning scenery, bracing winds of adventure, cozy nooks for resting when you are weary, and much more. I am your Guide, as well as your constant Companion. I know every step of the journey ahead of you, all the way to heaven.

You don't have to choose between staying close to Me and staying on course. Since *I am the Way*, staying close to Me is staying on course. As you focus your thoughts on Me, I will guide you carefully along today's journey. Don't worry about what is around the next bend. Just concentrate on enjoying My Presence and staying in step with Me.

*John 14:6; Colossians 4:2*

# Week 21

Instead of gazing into the unknown future, live each moment in joyful awareness of My Presence. I hold your future safely in My hands. It will unfurl before you as you go step by step through each day.

Dear Jesus,

I love this imagery. It reminds me of seeing red carpet rolled out in front of an honored person. I'm blessed by knowing that You hold my future safely in Your hands: releasing it to me moment by moment. Help me enjoy the wonder of Your Presence—accessible to me only in the present.

Beloved, I want to teach you how to spend more of your time in the present. The future, as most people conceptualize it, does not really exist. I hold it far beyond the reach of any person. When you or others gaze into the future, making predictions, you are simply exercising your imaginations. I alone have access to what is "not yet," because My existence isn't limited by time. As you go step by step through each day, I unroll the future before you. While you walk forward on the *red carpet* of time, you never set foot on anything but the present moment. Recognizing the futility of future-gazing can help set you free to live more fully in the present. The freer you become, the more you can enjoy the reality of My Presence.

Becoming free is a demanding process, because your mind is accustomed to wandering into the future at will. When you find yourself engaged in such thoughts, recognize that you are roaming in a fantasy land. As you awaken yourself with this truth, it's as if the ground drops out from under whatever you were fantasizing. This helps you return to the present, the here and now. I eagerly await you, ready to enfold you in My unfailing Love.

Since no man knows the future,
who can tell him what is to come?
*Ecclesiastes 8:7*

"I am the Alpha and the Omega," says the Lord God,
"who is, and who was, and who is to come, the Almighty."
*Revelation 1:8*

The LORD's unfailing love surrounds
the man who trusts in him.

*Psalm 32:10*

# Sunday

Y ou are on the path of My choosing. There is no randomness about your life. Here and Now comprise the coordinates of your daily life. Most people let their moments slip through their fingers, half-lived. They avoid the present by worrying about the future or longing for a better time and place. They forget that they are creatures who are subject to the limitations of time and space. They forget their Creator, who walks with them only in the present.

Every moment is alive with My glorious Presence, to those whose hearts are intimately connected with Mine. As you give yourself more and more to a life of constant communion with Me, you will find that you simply have no time for worry. Thus, you are freed to let My Spirit direct your steps, enabling you to walk along *the path of Peace.*

*Luke 12:25–26; Luke 1:79*

## Monday

Do not worry about tomorrow! This is not a suggestion, but a command. I divided time into days and nights, so that you would have manageable portions of life to handle. *My grace is sufficient for you*, but its sufficiency is for only one day at a time. When you worry about the future, you heap day upon day of troubles onto your flimsy frame. You stagger under this heavy load, which I never intended you to carry.

Throw off this oppressive burden with one quick thrust of trust. Anxious thoughts meander about and crisscross in your brain, but trusting Me brings you directly into My Presence. As you thus affirm your faith, shackles of worry fall off instantly. Enjoy My Presence continually by trusting Me at all times.

*Matthew 6:34; 2 Corinthians 12:9;*
*Psalm 62:8 (NKJV)*

## Tuesday

Rejoice in Me always! No matter what is going on, you can rejoice in your Love-relationship with Me. This is *the secret of being content in all circumstances*. So many people dream of the day when they will finally be happy: when they are out of debt, when their children are out of trouble, when they have more leisure time, and so on. While they daydream, their moments are trickling into the ground like precious balm spilling wastefully from overturned bottles.

Fantasizing about future happiness will never bring fulfillment, because fantasy is unreality. Even though I am invisible, I am far more Real than the world you see around you. My reality is eternal and unchanging. Bring your moments to Me, and I will fill them with vibrant Joy. *Now* is the time to rejoice in My Presence!

**Philippians 4:4, 12; Psalm 102:27**

## Wednesday

Let Me show you My way for you this day. I guide you continually, so you can relax and enjoy My Presence in the present. Living well is both a discipline and an art. Concentrate on staying close to Me, the divine Artist. Discipline your thoughts to trust Me as I work My ways in your life. Pray about everything; then, leave outcomes up to Me. Do not fear My will, for through it I accomplish what is best for you. Take a deep breath and dive into the depths of absolute trust in Me. *Underneath are the everlasting arms!*

*Psalm 5:2–3; Deuteronomy 33:27*

## Thursday

Trust Me and refuse to worry, for *I am your Strength and Song*. You are feeling wobbly this morning, looking at difficult times looming ahead, measuring them against your own strength. However, they are not today's tasks—or even tomorrow's. So leave them in the future and come home to the present, where you will find Me waiting for you. Since *I am your Strength*, I can empower you to handle each task as it comes. Because *I am your Song*, I can give you Joy as you work alongside Me.

Keep bringing your mind back to the present moment. Among all My creatures, only humans can anticipate future events. This ability is a blessing, but it becomes a curse whenever it is misused. If you use your magnificent mind to worry about tomorrow, you cloak yourself in dark unbelief. However, when the hope of heaven fills your thoughts, the Light of My Presence envelops you. Though heaven is future, it is also present tense. As you walk in the Light with Me, you have one foot on earth and one foot in heaven.

*Exodus 15:2; 2 Corinthians 10:5;*
*Hebrews 10:23*

## *Friday*

I am perpetually with you, taking care of you. That is the most important fact of your existence. I am not limited by time or space; My Presence with you is a forever-promise. You need not fear the future, for I am already there. When you make that *quantum leap* into eternity, you will find Me awaiting you in heaven. Your future is in My hands; I release it to you day by day, moment by moment. Therefore, *do not worry about tomorrow.*

I want you to live this day abundantly, seeing all there is to see, doing all there is to do. Don't be distracted by future concerns. Leave them to Me! Each day of life is a glorious gift, but so few people know how to live within the confines of today. Much of their energy for abundant living spills over the time line into tomorrow's worries or past regrets. Their remaining energy is sufficient only for limping through the day, not for living it to the full. I am training you to keep your focus on My Presence in the present. This is how to receive abundant Life, which flows freely from My throne of grace.

*Matthew 6:34; John 10:10; James 4:13–15*

*Saturday*

Anxiety is a result of envisioning the future without Me. So the best defense against worry is staying in communication with Me. When you turn your thoughts toward Me, you can think much more positively. Remember to listen, as well as to speak, making your thoughts a dialogue with Me.

If you must consider upcoming events, follow these rules: 1) Do not linger in the future, because anxieties sprout up like mushrooms when you wander there. 2) Remember the promise of My continual Presence; include Me in any imagery that comes to mind. This mental discipline does not come easily, because you are accustomed to being god of your fantasies. However, the reality of My Presence with you, now and forevermore, outshines any fantasy you could ever imagine.

*Luke 12:22–26; Ephesians 3:20–21*

# Week 22

> Living close to Me is a way of continual
> newness. I, the Creator of the universe, am
> more creative than you can imagine.

## Dear Jesus,

I love living close to You: It satisfies deep longings
in me. I confess, though, that I'm a creature of habit.
When I find a way of approaching You that works, I
stick with that method—making it part of my routine.
As I discover other means of drawing near to You, I
add them to my routine as well. This approach helps
me to be faithful in praying, but it is definitely not
a way of continual newness. I would like to be more
creative in my relationship with You, yet I don't want
to abandon my old ways completely.

Beloved, your desire to live close to Me delights My
heart. I'm also pleased that you are committed to
praying for people and situations on a regular basis. I
understand the tension you feel between being faithful
in your prayers and being creative. Because your mind is
both fallen and finite, you are not capable of continual
creativity. Your routine prayers help you cover a wide

range of praises and petitions without overtaxing your brain. But that very efficiency carries with it a danger: You can sleepwalk through your regular prayers. To avoid doing that, make use of the massive Power source within you—the Holy Spirit. He will help you stay alert, as you invite Him to empower your prayers with Life.

I'm not asking you to abandon your old ways of praying, but I *am* challenging you to seek new ways of communing with Me. You are capable of much more creativity than you realize, because I made you in My own image and put My Spirit within you. As you ponder ways to bring Me pleasure, I "tiptoe" closer to you. If you listen attentively, I will whisper some ideas in your mind. Seeking fresh ways to commune with Me will awaken your soul and enliven your relationship with Me.

In the beginning God created the heavens and the earth.
*Genesis 1:1*

And pray in the Spirit on all occasions with all kinds of prayers and requests. With this in mind, be alert and always keep on praying for all the saints.
*Ephesians 6:18*

For great is your love, reaching to the heavens; your faithfulness reaches to the skies. Be exalted, O God, above the heavens; let your glory be over all the earth.
*Psalm 57:10–11*

## Sunday

I speak to you continually. My nature is to communicate, though not always in words. I fling glorious sunsets across the sky, day after day after day. I speak in the faces and voices of loved ones. I caress you with a gentle breeze that refreshes and delights you. I speak softly in the depths of your spirit, where I have taken up residence.

You can find Me in each moment, when you have eyes that see and ears that hear. Ask My Spirit to sharpen your spiritual eyesight and hearing. I rejoice each time you discover My Presence. Practice looking and listening for Me during quiet intervals. Gradually you will find Me in more and more of your moments. *You will seek Me and find Me, when you seek Me above all else.*

*Psalm 8:1–4; Psalm 19:1–2;*
*1 Corinthians 6:19; Jeremiah 29:13*

## Monday

I am God with you, for all time and throughout eternity. Don't let the familiarity of that concept numb its impact on your consciousness. My perpetual Presence with you can be a continual source of Joy, springing up and flowing out in streams of abundant Life. Let your mind reverberate with meanings of My Names: Jesus—*the Lord saves*, and Emmanuel—*God with us*. Strive to remain conscious of My Presence even in your busiest moments. Talk with Me about whatever delights you, whatever upsets you, whatever is on your mind. These tiny steps of daily discipline, taken one after the other, will keep you close to Me on the path of Life.

*Matthew 1:21, 23; Acts 2:28*

## Tuesday

Open your hands and your heart to receive this day as a precious gift from Me. I begin each day with a sunrise, announcing My radiant Presence. By the time you rise from your bed, I have already prepared the way before you. I eagerly await your first conscious thought. I rejoice when you glance My way.

Bring Me the gift of thanksgiving, which opens your heart to rich communion with Me. Because I am God, from whom all blessings flow, thankfulness is the best way to draw near Me. Sing praise songs to Me; tell of My wondrous works. Remember that *I take great delight in you; I rejoice over you with singing.*

**Psalm 118:24; Psalm 95:2; Zephaniah 3:17**

# *Wednesday*

As you listen to birds calling to one another, hear also My Love-call to you. I speak to you continually: through sights, sounds, thoughts, impressions, Scripture. There is no limit to the variety of ways I can communicate with you. Your part is to be attentive to My messages, in whatever form they come. When you set out to find Me in a day, you discover that the world is vibrantly alive with My Presence. You can find Me not only in beauty and birdcalls, but also in tragedy and faces filled with grief. I can take the deepest sorrow and *weave it into a pattern for good.*

Search for Me and My messages as you go through this day. *You will seek Me and find Me when you seek Me with your whole being.*

*John 10:27; Romans 8:28 (AMP);*
*Jeremiah 29:13*

# Thursday

Stay ever so close to Me, and you will not deviate from the path I have prepared for you. This is the most efficient way to stay on track; it is also the most enjoyable way. Men tend to multiply duties in their observance of religion. This practice enables them to give Me money, time, and work without yielding up to Me what I desire the most—their hearts. Rules can be observed mechanically. Once they become habitual, they can be followed with minimal effort and almost no thought. These habit-forming rules provide a false sense of security, lulling the soul into a comatose condition.

What I search for in My children is an awakened soul that thrills to the Joy of My Presence! I created mankind to glorify Me and enjoy Me forever. I provide the Joy; your part is to glorify Me by living close to Me.

*Deuteronomy 6:5; Colossians 3:23;*
*Psalm 16:11*

## Friday

Thank Me throughout this day for My Presence and My Peace. These are gifts of supernatural proportions. Ever since the resurrection, I have comforted My followers with these messages: *Peace be with you,* and *I am with you always.* Listen as I offer you My Peace and Presence in full measure. The best way to receive these glorious gifts is to thank Me for them.

It is impossible to spend too much time thanking and praising Me. I created you first and foremost to glorify Me. Thanksgiving and praise put you in proper relationship with Me, opening the way for My riches to flow into you. As you thank Me for My Presence and Peace, you appropriate My richest gifts.

*Luke 24:36; Matthew 28:20; Hebrews 13:15*

*Saturday*

As you sit quietly in My Presence, let Me fill your heart and mind with thankfulness. This is the most direct way to achieve a thankful stance. If your mind needs a focal point, gaze at My Love poured out for you on the cross. Remember that *nothing in heaven or on earth can separate you from that Love.* This remembrance builds a foundation of gratitude in you, a foundation that circumstances cannot shake.

As you go through this day, look for tiny treasures strategically placed along the way. I lovingly go before you and plant little pleasures to brighten your day. Look carefully for them, and pluck them one by one. When you reach the end of the day, you will have gathered a lovely bouquet. Offer it up to Me with a grateful heart. Receive My Peace as you lie down to sleep, with thankful thoughts playing a lullaby in your mind.

*Romans 8:38–39; Psalm 4:7–8*

# Week 23

> I have awakened in your heart strong desire to know Me. This longing originated in Me, though it now burns brightly in you.

## Dear Jesus,

Thank You for awakening my heart! Before I knew You, I tried to find life in many different places. Often I would think I had found what I was searching for—only to be disappointed later. After I became thoroughly disillusioned, You reached down and took me into Your own family. Years later, I began thirsting for You: longing to know You at a deeper heart level. I set aside time to meet with You as my living God— vibrantly present with me.

Beloved, when you set out to know Me more intimately, I rejoiced but I wasn't surprised. I had been pursuing you long before you began your quest. I was working in your life experiences, as well as in your heart, mind, and spirit. Your desire for a closer walk with Me grew out of My painstaking work in you. I initiated your longing for Me, and your response delights Me.

It is important for you to know Me as the Initiator in our relationship. If you think it is your spiritual disciplines that keep you close to Me, you are at risk. Some days you may skimp on your time with Me or not be able to concentrate well. If you're depending on your own efforts to stay near Me, you will feel distant from Me at such times. But if you are relying on Me—what I have done, am doing, will do—you know My Love for you is always assured. So you can rest in Me: trusting in My unfailing Love, flourishing in My abiding Presence.

Above all else, guard your heart, for it is the wellspring of life.
*Proverbs 4:23*

My soul thirsts for God, for the living God.
When can I go and meet with God?
*Psalm 42:2*

I am the vine, you are the branches; he who abides in Me, and I in him, he bears much fruit, for apart from Me you can do nothing.
*John 15:5 NASB*

But I am like an olive tree flourishing in the house of God;
I trust in God's unfailing love for ever and ever.
*Psalm 52:8*

# Sunday

This is a time of abundance in your life. *Your cup runneth over* with blessings. After plodding uphill for many weeks, you are now traipsing through lush meadows drenched in warm sunshine. I want you to enjoy to the full this time of ease and refreshment. I delight in providing it for you.

Sometimes My children hesitate to receive My good gifts with open hands. Feelings of false guilt creep in, telling them they don't deserve to be so richly blessed. This is nonsense-thinking, because no one deserves anything from Me. My kingdom is not about earning and deserving; it's about believing and receiving.

When a child of Mine balks at accepting My gifts, I am deeply grieved. When you receive My abundant blessings with a grateful heart, I rejoice. My pleasure in giving and your pleasure in receiving flow together in joyous harmony.

*Psalm 23:5 (KJV); John 3:16;*
*Luke 11:9–10; Romans 8:32*

# Monday

Never take for granted My intimate nearness. Marvel at the wonder of My continual Presence with you. Even the most ardent human lover cannot be with you always. Nor can another person know the intimacies of your heart, mind, and spirit. *I know everything about you—even to the number of hairs on your head.* You don't need to work at revealing yourself to Me.

Many people spend a lifetime or a small fortune searching for someone who understands them. Yet I am freely available to all who call upon My Name, who open their hearts to receive Me as Savior. This simple act of faith is the beginning of a lifelong love story. I, the Lover of your soul, understand you perfectly and love you eternally.

*Luke 12:7; John 1:12; Romans 10:13*

## Tuesday

*I have loved you with an everlasting Love.* Before time began, I knew you. For years you swam around in a sea of meaninglessness, searching for Love, hoping for hope. All that time I was pursuing you, aching to embrace you in My compassionate arms.

When time was right, I revealed Myself to you. I lifted you out of that sea of despair and set you down on a firm foundation. Sometimes you felt naked—exposed to the revealing Light of My Presence. I wrapped an ermine robe around you: *My robe of righteousness.* I sang you a Love song, whose beginning and end are veiled in eternity. I infused meaning into your mind and harmony into your heart. Join Me in singing My song. Together we will draw others *out of darkness into My marvelous Light.*

*Jeremiah 31:3; Isaiah 61:10;*
*1 Peter 2:9 (NKJV)*

## Wednesday

Grow strong in the Light of My Presence. As My Face shines upon you, you receive nutrients that enhance your growth in grace. I designed you to commune with Me face to Face, and this interaction strengthens your soul. Such communion provides a tiny glimpse of what awaits you in heaven, where all barriers between you and My Glory will be removed. This meditative time with Me blesses you doubly. You experience My Presence here and now, and you are refreshed by the hope of heaven, where you will know Me in ecstatic Joy.

*Psalm 4:6–8; Revelation 21:23*

## Thursday

I am with you and all around you, encircling you in golden rays of Light. I always behold you Face to face. Not one of your thoughts escapes My notice. Because I am infinite, I am able to love you as if you and I were the only ones in the universe.

Walk with Me in intimate Love-steps, but do not lose sight of My Majesty. I desire to be your closest Friend, yet I am also your sovereign Lord. I created your brain with capacity to know Me as Friend and Lord simultaneously. The human mind is the pinnacle of My creation, but so few use it for its primary purpose— knowing Me. I communicate continually through My Spirit, My Word, and My creation. Only humans are capable of receiving Me and responding to My Presence. You are indeed *fearfully and wonderfully made!*

*Psalm 34:4–7; 2 Peter 1:16–17;*
*John 17:3; Psalm 139:14*

## Friday

Meet Me in early morning splendor. I eagerly await you here. In the stillness of this holy time with Me, *I renew your strength* and saturate you with Peace. While others turn over for extra sleep or anxiously tune in to the latest news, you commune with the Creator of the universe. I have awakened in your heart strong desire to know Me. This longing originated in Me, though it now burns brightly in you.

When you seek My Face in response to My Love-call, both of us are blessed. This is a deep mystery, designed more for your enjoyment than for your understanding. I am not a dour God who discourages pleasure. I delight in your enjoyment of *everything that is true, noble, right, pure, lovely, admirable. Think on these things*, and My Light in you will shine brighter day by day.

*Isaiah 40:31; Psalm 27:4; Philippians 4:8*

I am creating something new in you: a bubbling spring of Joy that spills over into others' lives. Do not mistake this Joy for your own or try to take credit for it in any way. Instead, watch in delight as My Spirit flows through you to bless others. Let yourself become a reservoir of the Spirit's fruit.

Your part is to live close to Me, open to all that I am doing in you. Don't try to control the streaming of My Spirit through you. Just keep focusing on Me as we walk through this day together. Enjoy My Presence, which permeates you with *Love, Joy, and Peace.*

**John 3:8; Galatians 5:22**

# Week 24

Listen to Me even while you are listening
to other people. As they open their souls
to your scrutiny, you are on holy ground.
You need the help of My Spirit
to respond appropriately.

*Dear Jesus,*

This is an area where I really want to grow. When
people open up to me, I get so focused on them and
what they're saying that I forget to listen to You. The
latent hero in me tries to take charge of the situation and
rescue the other person. While I'm listening, my mind is
analyzing data: searching for solutions. The main problem
with this approach is that I'm relying on myself—trusting
in my own abilities, which are totally inadequate.

*Beloved,* it's good that you recognize your tendency
to play the hero. It's even better that you want to
grow out of this role. When people bare their souls to
you, you are indeed on holy ground. Your responsibility
is to listen and love. If you jump in with both feet—
trying to rescue them—your muddy footprints pollute
the holy terrain. Some people will retreat when this

happens; others may be too wounded to realize they've been violated. Either way, you have missed the mark and spoiled a splendid opportunity.

To function effectively on holy ground, you need the help of the Holy Spirit. Ask Him to think through you, listen through you, love through you. As the Spirit's Love shines through you, My healing Presence goes to work in the other person. While you continue listening, I will sometimes give you words of wisdom to share. But your main role is to direct the person toward Me and My limitless resources.

If you follow these guidelines, both you and others will be blessed. They will connect with My unfailing Love at soul-level. My Spirit will flow through you delightfully—refreshing your soul. You may not feel heroic, but your soul will feel satisfied.

"Do not come any closer," God said. "Take off your sandals,
for the place where you are standing is holy ground."
*Exodus 3:5*

Let the morning bring me word of your unfailing love,
for I have put my trust in you. Show me the way
I should go, for to you I lift up my soul.
*Psalm 143:8*

My soul will be satisfied as with the richest of foods....
*Psalm 63:5*

## Sunday

Learn to relate to others through My Love rather than yours. Your human love is ever so limited, full of flaws and manipulation. My loving Presence, which always enfolds you, is available to bless others as well as you. Instead of trying harder to help people through your own paltry supplies, become aware of My unlimited supply, which is accessible to you continually. Let My Love envelop your outreach to other people.

Many of My precious children have fallen prey to burnout. A better description of their condition might be "drainout." Countless interactions with needy people have drained them, without their conscious awareness. You are among these weary ones, who are like wounded soldiers needing R&R. Take time to rest in the Love-Light of My Presence. I will gradually restore to you the energy that you have lost over the years. *Come to Me, all you who are weary and burdened, and you will find rest for your souls.*

*Exodus 33:14; Matthew 11:28–29*

# Monday

Come to Me, and rest in My Peace. My Face is shining upon you, in rays of *Peace transcending understanding.* Instead of trying to figure things out yourself, you can relax in the Presence of the One who knows everything. As you lean on Me in trusting dependence, you feel peaceful and complete. This is how I designed you to live: in close communion with Me.

When you are around other people, you tend to cater to their expectations—real or imagined. You feel enslaved to pleasing them, and your awareness of My Presence grows dim. Your efforts to win their approval eventually exhaust you. You offer these people dry crumbs rather than the *living water* of My Spirit flowing through you. This is not My way for you! Stay in touch with Me, even during your busiest moments. Let My Spirit give you words of grace as you live in the Light of My Peace.

*Philippians 4:6–7; John 7:38;*
*Ephesians 5:18–20*

## Tuesday

Find freedom through seeking to please Me above all else. *You can have only one Master.* When you let others' expectations drive you, you scatter your energy to the winds. Your own desire to look good can also drain your energy. I am your Master, and I do not drive you to be what you are not. Your pretense displeases Me, especially when it is in My "service." Concentrate on staying close to Me at all times. It is impossible to be inauthentic while you are focusing on My Presence.

*Ephesians 5:8–10; Matthew 23:8;*
*Matthew 6:1*

## Wednesday

Live first and foremost in My Presence. Gradually you will become more aware of Me than of people and places around you. This awareness will not detract from your relationships with others. Instead, it will increase your ability to give love and encouragement to them. My Peace will permeate your words and demeanor. You will be active in the world, yet one step removed from it. You will not be easily shaken, because My enveloping Presence buffers the blow of problems.

This is the path I have set before you. As you follow it wholeheartedly, you experience abundant Life and Peace.

*Psalm 89:15–16; Psalm 16:8;*
*2 Peter 1:2*

# Thursday

I speak to you from the depths of your being. Hear Me saying soothing words of Peace, assuring you of My Love. Do not listen to voices of accusation, for they are not from Me. I speak to you in love-tones, lifting you up. My Spirit convicts cleanly, without crushing words of shame. Let the Spirit take charge of your mind, combing out tangles of deception. Be transformed by the truth that I live within you.

The Light of My Presence is shining upon you, in benedictions of Peace. Let My Light shine in you; don't dim it with worries or fears. Holiness is letting Me live through you. Since I dwell in you, you are fully equipped to be holy. Pause before responding to people or situations, giving My Spirit space to act through you. Hasty words and actions leave no room for Me; this is atheistic living. I want to inhabit all your moments—gracing your thoughts, words, and behavior.

*Romans 8:1–2; Colossians 1:27;*
*1 Corinthians 6:19*

# Friday

Watch your words diligently. Words have such great power to bless or to wound. When you speak carelessly or negatively, you damage others as well as yourself. This ability to verbalize is an awesome privilege, granted only to those I created in My image. You need help in wielding this mighty power responsibly.

Though the world applauds quick-witted retorts, My instructions about communication are quite different: *Be quick to listen, slow to speak, and slow to become angry.* Ask My Spirit to help you whenever you speak. I have trained you to pray—"Help me, Holy Spirit"—before answering the phone, and you have seen the benefits of this discipline. Simply apply the same discipline to communicating with people around you. If they are silent, pray before speaking to them. If they are talking, pray before responding. These are split-second prayers, but they put you in touch with My Presence. In this way, your speaking comes under the control of My Spirit. As positive speech patterns replace your negative ones, the increase in your Joy will amaze you.

**Proverbs 12:18; James 1:19; Ephesians 4:29**

## Saturday

Learn to listen to Me even while you are listening to other people. As they open their souls to your scrutiny, *you are on holy ground.* You need the help of My Spirit to respond appropriately. Ask Him to think through you, live through you, love through you. My own Being is alive within you in the Person of the Holy Spirit. If you respond to others' needs through your unaided thought processes, you offer them dry crumbs. When the Spirit empowers your listening and speaking, My *streams of living water flow* through you to other people. Be a channel of My Love, Joy, and Peace by listening to Me as you listen to others.

*Exodus 3:5; 1 Corinthians 6:19;*
*John 7:38–39*

# Prayers

# Prayers

_____
_____
_____
_____
_____
_____
_____
_____
_____
_____
_____
_____
_____

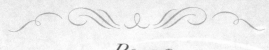

## Prayers

_____

_____

_____

_____

_____

_____

_____

_____

_____

_____

_____

_____

# Prayers

_____

_____

_____

_____

_____

_____

_____

_____

_____

_____

_____

## Prayers

_____

_____

_____

_____

_____

_____

_____

_____

_____

_____

_____

_____

# Prayers

_____

_____

_____

_____

_____

_____

_____

_____

_____

_____

_____

# Prayers

# About the Author

Sarah Young's best-selling devotional writing in *Jesus Calling* and *Dear Jesus*—highlighted here in this exclusive, limited edition—is helping untold numbers of people in their quest for intimacy with Christ.

Sarah has a degree in philosophy from Wellesley College and holds graduate degrees in psychology/counseling from Tufts University, Georgia State University, and Covenant Theological Seminary.

She and her husband have traveled widely, counseling and planting churches in Japan and Australia. They currently minister to Japanese people living in Perth, Australia.